EDNA ST. VINCENT MILLAY

AMERICA'S BEST-LOVED POET

EDNA ST. VINCENT MILLAY

AMERICA'S BEST-LOVED POET

(February 22, 1892 — October 19, 1950)

→»→»→»《←‹←‹←‹←

by TOBY SHAFTER

→»→»→»《←‹←‹←‹←

JULIAN MESSNER, INC.

New York

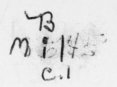

Published by Julian Messner, Inc.
8 West 40 Street, New York 18

Published simultaneously in Canada
by The Copp Clark Publishing Co. Limited

Printed in the United States of America
Library of Congress Catalog Card No. 57—6838

"Forest Trees" by Vincent Millay from *St. Nicholas Magazine*. Reprinted by permission of the publishers Appleton-Century-Crofts, Inc.

"The Land of Romance" by E. Vincent Millay from *St. Nicholas Magazine*. Reprinted by permission of the publishers Appleton-Century-Crofts, Inc.

"Hope" by Edna von der Heide from *St. Nicholas Magazine*. Copyright, 1910, Century Company. Reprinted by permission of the publishers Appleton-Century-Crofts, Inc.

The Dishpan Song and *Circus Rag* reprinted by permission of Norma Millay.

Letter No. 9 from *Letters of Edna St. Vincent Millay* reprinted by permission of Norma Millay.

The letter from Arthur Davison Ficke to Ferdinand Earle reprinted by permission of Mrs. Arthur Davison Ficke.

In Memory of My Parents

Acknowledgments

435

Since this is the first biography of the major part of the life of Edna St. Vincent Millay, printed sources of information were necessarily limited. The research for the early years was made possible through the cooperation of friends and relatives (in the Knox County area of Maine) who were kind enough to share their recollection of "Vincent" with me. These, together with scattered newspaper clippings, old school magazines, occasional magazine articles and reviews, formed the basis of my research.

In Camden, Maine, Corinne Sawyer, a classmate of Edna St. Vincent Millay, spent many hours with me and was especially cooperative and sympathetic to the project. She and Mrs. Doris Ogier Pitcher, the librarian, put at my disposal the facilities of the Camden Public Library. I was especially fortunate in that, during the course of my work there, they were able to assemble an increasing accumulation of material on the subject.

Mrs. Stella Lenfest, another classmate, assisted me with her memories of high school days and after. I also interviewed the late Mrs. Elmore, Mrs. Willard Chapin, Sr., Jessie Osmer, Walter Conley and the Hurlburts. The Edna St. Vincent Millay week, which George Perry organized in Camden in August, 1953, was most helpful to the work.

At the offices of the Camden *Herald*, I read through the back newspaper files for the ten year period beginning with 1902, trying to recapture the atmosphere of the time that led to the fascinating events of Edna St. Vincent Millay's life.

The late Percy Keller of Camden, a cousin of the poet's mother, supplied me with information upon several occasions. Mrs. Annie Burns of Union, a niece of the poet's father, was of great assistance.

In New York, Harrison Dowd described for me many of the events of Edna St. Vincent Millay's life there and abroad. Deems Taylor recounted several interesting anecdotes about the poet.

The incomparable *Letters of Edna St. Vincent Millay* were invaluable in marshaling not only the facts but the feelings of the poet through most of her adult life. The impressive body of Edna St. Vincent Millay's work—her poetry, plays and prose writing—served as a constant inspiration and were perhaps the most important spur to any biographer, even in such a modest effort as this.

I spent a wholly delightful day in May at Steepletop with Norma Millay and Charles Ellis, her husband. I am most grateful to Norma Millay for reading this book before publication.

Finally, I wish to thank Frances Park who graciously undertook to read the galley proof with me.

T. S.

EDNA ST. VINCENT MILLAY

AMERICA'S BEST-LOVED POET

ONE

Tongues buzzed in Camden, Maine. A new family had come to town. And a strange family it was, too. "There's just her and the three girls," the men said as they bent over the lobster traps they were mending. "Wonder whether she is a widow woman."

"It's hard to bring up three children without a man around," the women told one another over their clicking knitting needles. "In Union, they say she told her husband to leave because he gambled. He went down east—just like that. Now she goes out nursing. Makes hair switches, too. Turns her hand to most anything to make a living for the three young ones."

Unmindful of the interest, the new Millay family went about its business of settling down in Camden. Mother Millay was glad to be back in the small seaside town with its blue hills and island-dotted bay. Maine was her home—come what may—and the home of her ancestors and progeny.

They found a house a short distance from the village. It was near the mill—in the section known as Millville—but it nestled cozily in a sun-struck hollow, and a swift-running stream ran behind it. No matter that the house was unpainted or that the room in the basement had floor boards laid directly on the ground. The stoves throughout the house presaged the winter cold seeping through weathered clapboards, but now it was only nearing the fall of the year. The meadow in front of the house sloped down toward the brook, its tall timothy grass waving silvery fronds between the abundant staffs of goldenrod and mustard seed and Queen Anne's lace, with the widespread burdock bushes crowding rudely in.

It was a good place for three small girls to play. The two older girls, Vincent and Norma—their long red hair streaming in the sun—rushed headlong to throw themselves into the cool water of the brook. Vincent, who was twelve, had already learned to swim in the few short weeks they had spent in Camden. Her thin arms frantically churned the water in a dog paddle and her legs flailed against the current. Though she wound her copper-red hair high on her head, a few ringlets escaped and hung damply about her frail neck when she emerged. The faded cotton dress and bloomers she wore as a bathing suit clung to her small frame and her teeth chattered a bit in spite of the warm rays of the August sun. Norma, a sturdy girl of ten, stood waist high in the brook, splashing the water.

"Vincent! Vincent!" she cried. "Am I swimming now? I'm only touching bottom with one foot."

"No, no," Vincent shouted. "Float off! Float off with both feet and kick, kick, kick." Vincent once more rushed impetuously into the water to demonstrate.

"Now swim toward me, Norma," she commanded, "and take both feet off the bottom. Swim now, swim now, swim toward me." There was almost a bewitching quality in Vincent's narrowed gray-green eyes as she wheedled her young sister off her feet.

Norma advanced in a storm of splashing foam and then ph-fut! Down she went and came up sputtering. Vincent capered around her gleefully.

"You were swimming! You were swimming! You swam five strokes." Vincent slithered downstream in the water with not much more motion than a fish.

Norma stood coughing until her face was flushed as pink
as her hair. Then she tried again and again. Each time after
swimming four or five strokes, Norma went under. But she
was a robust child, her spirit as sturdy as her body. She
practiced long and hard and soon she was swimming
vigorously.

Kathleen, the little sister who was only eight, stood on the
bank and pretended that she was swimming in the long
meadow grass. "See how I swim! See how I swim!" she
called out.

Vincent and Norma laughed at her. Kathleen shook her
dark head and looked at them dolefully.

Tired of their water games, Vincent and Norma joined
Kathleen in their dripping cotton dresses. All three raced
around in the tall timothy grass.

The sun was already low when Norma shouted, "Last one
in the house is a pickled lime!" Vincent and Kathleen ran
after Norma toward the unpainted, weather-beaten house at
the end of the lane.

The three girls tumbled up the back steps to the kitchen.
Norma was first, Vincent was second and Kathleen was the
pickled lime. The kitchen was dim and cheerless. In one
corner was a rusting iron sink with a cold-water tap. Next
to it stood an old-fashioned oak icebox. The pan underneath
had overflowed and there was a spreading puddle on the
worn piece of linoleum that ran down the middle toward
the huge, black iron stove.

Vincent darted toward the icebox. She lifted the hinged
board at the bottom and in a moment she had run into the
back yard with the overflowing pan. There she emptied the
water with a quick flourish. When she returned to the
kitchen Norma was already mopping the floor. In a few
moments the kitchen floor was gleaming—though damp.
Vincent surveyed it with satisfaction. "We won't have to

wash the floor for another whole week," she observed, "unless the icebox pan overflows again."

"I'm hungry," Kathleen announced. "Is Mother coming home for supper?"

Vincent clapped her hand over her mouth. "I forgot all about supper," she exclaimed. "And mother is not coming home."

Kathleen's face fell. She knew that when Mother Millay did not return from a nursing case, the food would be cold leftovers or strangely concocted dishes. Anything that popped into Vincent's mind might arrive on the table in the guise of supper. Kathleen much preferred to have her mother stay at home—as other mothers did. Though Mother Millay was usually preoccupied even at home with the plaiting and weaving of hair switches, there were good things to eat. The hot things were hot and the cold things were cold as they were supposed to be, and nothing was burnt.

Vincent was rummaging in the icebox. She found the remains of a pot of baked beans, butter but no bread, a bit of stale cake and almost an entire jar of pickles. She laid these carefully on the table. After more searching, she at last brought out the end of a loaf of bread.

"Here's bread to put the butter on," she told them triumphantly. "Norma, you bring the mugs to the table."

"What are we going to put in them?" Norma asked.

"Oh, I forgot to get milk today," Vincent gasped. "I'll start a fire in the stove in a jiffy and we'll all have hot tea."

She went to the woodshed and returned with an armful of kindling wood. She crumpled old newspapers in the grate of the iron stove, threw on a few sticks, and soon there was a merry blaze and a bubbling kettleful of water.

When the three little girls had eaten their fill of baked beans and pickles and strong, hot tea, the new home seemed a cheerful place.

TWO

Camden was a fine town for a twelve-year-old—as Vincent was—the summer of 1904. There was a wharf to play on during foggy weather. Sometimes at low tide it was fun to climb underneath and go from one green, slime-covered pile to the next. The fairy world of green castles and gardens underneath the water was wonderful to see. The salt water stung Vincent's eyes when she opened them under water, but she always held them open as long as she could. Looking at the cities under the sea was worth a pair of stinging, red-rimmed eyes.

On sunny days there was the Atlantic Ocean that came rolling into Penobscot Bay to swim in, too. When Vincent swam in the ocean it was not from a tame sand beach. She dived into the water straight from the high rock ledges that overhung the waves at high tide.

Best of all, there was the mountain. The back trail to the mountain was just down the street from the little house in the hollow, and Vincent climbed it several times a week.

"I'm going up the mountain," she said airily to Norma this bright day. "Now you stay here and mind Kathleen."

"I want to go, too," Norma protested. "Let's take Kathleen."

"No. Kathleen is only eight years old. She is too little to climb the mountain," Vincent said firmly.

"But I am ten! I am ten and a half!" Norma insisted. "Let me go."

"No. Someone must mind Kathleen. Mother said so, and I have done it nearly all day. Don't you realize a person likes to get away from you young ones sometimes? I want to go to the mountain alone." For Vincent the issue was settled. Norma stood pouting.

"Here. Here's some money, Norma," said Vincent quickly. "Take Kathleen downstreet with you to the bakery and buy a date pie and a quart of milk for supper. Won't that be fun?"

At the mention of date pie, both Norma and Kathleen beamed. Forgotten was the mountain. Vincent danced off down the street like a copper-haired sprite, touching all the flowers lightly. Hand in hand with Kathleen, clutching the money tightly in her fist, Norma followed more sedately. At the crossroad Vincent skipped off to the left on her way to the mountain while her younger sisters continued straight down the street toward the town.

Vincent picked her way across the quiet streets with their well-kept square lawns and tidy white houses. Soon she reached the Mount Battie Trail. At the beginning, Mount Battie seemed scarcely a mountain at all, for a wide road went from the street up to a deceptively easy slope. It was a favorite woodcutter's spot. Vincent's small figure balanced easily here and there on the untrimmed logs that were lying about. Then the road narrowed to a footpath. The footpath wound through the woods in ever steeper ascent. As the woods grew sparser, the trees became dwarfed and storm twisted.

Now Vincent was at the halfway mark—a grassy plateau with one weathered pine tree, small and gnarled. This was her favorite spot. From where she stood, Vincent could look down onto the blue bay and see the tiny wooded islands there. When she turned and looked the other way, there was a long, low mountain range almost lost in the mist. Vincent stood and breathed deep of the clear mountain air freshened by the sea breeze. It was so beautiful—almost more beauty than she could bear. She flung herself into the tall grass and looked up into the flawless blue sky. White, fleecy clouds floated by. She narrowed her eyes into slits until she could see only the limitless blue. Then it seemed that she, too, was floating. She lay there a long time—motionless. The sun faded behind the blue hills. There was a shadow on the mountain where she lay.

Vincent roused herself and stood indecisively in the tall grass. The wind blew her red hair and pressed her cotton dress against her body. There was a worried frown on her high forehead. Was there time to climb past the cliff above the timber line to gather berries before nightfall? She decided to chance it.

Sure-footed as a young doe, she made her way up on the surface of the huge bare boulders. Blueberry bushes grew thickly between the crevices. She scooped the plump berries into her pockets. When they were full to overflowing, she made a cloth shell of her handkerchief by knotting the corners.

Going down the mountain was harder than climbing up. Before, when she had scrambled up over the boulders, the crevices served as footholds. Now she had to thread her way around the huge rocks or make a clear jump from them. And in her hands, she clasped the handkerchief full of berries. The brambles scratched her arms and legs. She was afraid she might fall forward and roll down the mountain side.

Suddenly Vincent stopped short. She was on top of a steep cliff. Straight below her was a sheer drop of about twenty-five feet. The ledge on which she stood was ridged and narrow. She was in a kind of hollow. Above her towered a boulder, smooth and steep. She could go neither forward nor backward.

She envisioned herself spending the night here—or dying of starvation after many days of being lost and helpless. Vincent stopped herself. These wild fancies must end.

"I must think. I must think of a way of getting down." Sobbing softly, Vincent repeated over and over again to herself, "I went to the right." Perhaps, just perhaps, if I had turned left I might have found the trail, she thought desperately.

First she had to climb out of this imprisoning hollow. She wove her way, now left and then right, back up the mountain. With the sheer cliff well behind her, she zigzagged downward to the left. And then she found the trail again.

She paused to see the view once more from her favorite spot at the halfway mark. Looking down she could see the broad stand of maple. The fresh green leaves, shifting in the slight breeze, framed the doll-like town below. She could even pick out the tiny house in the hollow that was her new home. The brook that ran beside it looked like a wide blue penciled line winding through the fields of green.

It was almost dusk when Vincent reached home. Kathleen and Norma were peering anxiously out of the dimly lighted kitchen window. Vincent stepped softly across the threshhold. Two candles were burning. A low bowl of black-eyed Susans sat on the table. The room looked neat and cozy.

"Mummy was home for a while this afternoon," her two younger sisters greeted Vincent. "She ate two pieces of date pie."

"We waited supper for you," Norma continued.

"And she told us not to try to light the kerosene lamp by ourselves, so we used candles," Kathleen said all in one breath. "Now can we eat?"

Vincent's heart welled up with tenderness. Her little sisters were so good and loyal. They accepted all her dictums—good and bad. She resolved to take them on an excursion. Perhaps they could all take the electric trolley to Rockland and walk out on the breakwater to see the lighthouse. Or they might hike to Lake Megunticook for an all-day picnic. The mountain was her private place. She did not yet want her little sisters trailing after her there. When they were older and understood more, then she could take them.

"Look what I've brought you," Vincent cried, forcibly changing her mood. She held up the cupped handkerchief full of blueberries for them to see. She emptied her pockets into a large bowl. They all began removing the stems and leaves and washed the berries clean.

"We can have these for supper with milk and you may each have a big piece of date pie," Vincent planned, still remorseful and wanting to make them happy. "And after supper I'll tell you a story."

Vincent quickly set three soup plates on the oilcloth that covered the kitchen table. In the flickering candlelight she dished out the blueberries and poured milk over them. She cut generous slices of date pie for Norma and Kathleen and a somewhat smaller share for herself. The two younger sisters ate hungrily and silently. Vincent was silent but contemplative—scarcely interested in the food before her, though she had not eaten anything except a few blueberries on the mountain since early afternoon.

After the meal they all went upstairs to the third floor where the bedrooms were. The furniture was meager. The iron bedsteads had hard mattresses. A kerosene lamp threw enough light for Norma and Kathleen to undress and get into their nightgowns.

The two younger girls tucked themselves into bed. Vincent came into the room and sat down on the floor beside them. In a low, dramatic voice she told them thrilling tales of romance and danger. She told them quiet stories about flowers and weeds and hills. She even sang snatches of song and verse. After a time, Vincent realized it was strangely quiet. Both Norma and Kathleen were sleeping soundly.

She tiptoed downstairs to the sitting room. It was difficult to read by candlelight, but she found a book of poems that she knew almost by heart. Its binding was shabby and its pages dog eared. In it were some of the poems that Vincent loved best. Between the pages were little scraps of paper. On them Vincent had written poems of her own. Here was the one she had written about a bird when she was only seven years old.

More scraps of paper fluttered out like leaves falling to the ground. Vincent gathered them up carefully and read each one. Sometimes she changed a word. Occasionally she added a new line or ruthlessly crossed out stanza after stanza.

One poem particularly pleased her. She read it aloud twice. Then rummaging in the drawer of the table at which she sat, she brought out a yellow pad of paper. She painstakingly copied out the poem, printing each word in pencil and adding color decorations in crayon in the margins. When she had finished, she surveyed her work with satisfaction and tucked it away carefully in the drawer to show her mother.

She made a few idle lines and crosses. More than anything else now, she wanted to write a poem about the way she had felt on the mountain, but the words did not come. The few words she had written did not really tell how wonderful it was. Most of her poems were about the birds and the flowers and the woods, but someday she would write a poem about the mountain. It must be a poem like the mountain—immense and overwhelming. Now perhaps she could write a little poem about a hill, an afternoon on a hill.

She whispered rhyming words softly to herself. "Sun. One. Rise. Wise. Town. Down." Ever since she was a tiny girl—not more than three years old—she had played this game. "These words match," she would call out to her mother.

Now she began again. She wrote lines and scattered words, but she was not satisfied. Suddenly she crumpled up the paper and let it fall to the floor. She knew she would remember the good lines and the good words. The dross would fall away, and later she could write the poem again.

Vincent yawned. Her thin form slumped over the table. With one final effort, she went about the room blowing out the candles. Slipping off her thin cotton dress, she dropped to sleep on the bed in the next room.

THREE

So the summer passed. The Millay children romped and played in the meadow surrounding their little house. Mother Millay came home each afternoon in the break of her nursing duties to take a short nap and tidy the rooms. She rarely scolded the girls for not sweeping the floors, and she picked up the books and papers that Vincent left about without a word. She was gay and sprightly though she worked so hard.

When she had no case to nurse, Mother Millay stayed at home and plaited long hair into switches and transformations. Vincent fancied that when her mother was weaving at the wooden frame—her small dark head nodding and her large gray eyes intent on her work—she was sitting at a harp. The frame with its strands of hair hanging down at an angle did look like a harp with Mother Millay's sensitive hands strumming back and forth across the strings. The hair made a twanging sound as she worked. Often she sang sad songs or soft lullabies. Vincent sometimes put her own words to her mother's wordless humming. Vincent hated the "wigs" as she impolitely called the transformations. Though she liked to watch her mother make the elaborately curled "hair pieces" that the ladies of that decade used to wear, nothing could induce her to touch the "dead" hair herself.

While Mother Millay was at home they all had a gay and interesting time. They read poems together and sang as they washed dishes or gathered the frothy Queen Anne's lace in huge bouquets for every room in the house.

There were only a few weeks before the beginning of school. Entering a new school was always exciting.

"I wonder if the Camden school will be as large as the one in Rockport?" Norma mused.

"Oh, larger," Vincent assured her.

"Larger even than the Newburyport school?" Norma asked.

"No. Probably not as large as that one," Vincent replied judiciously.

"We've been to so many schools," little Kathleen put in. "Did you ever go to the same school twice in a row?"

Norma and Vincent counted the schools they had attended. "One. Two. Three. Did we go to school in Rockport when we lived there the year before last? Four. Five. I think we went to two or three different schools in Massachusetts when we lived there."

"And we've gone to nearly all the schools around here in Knox County in Maine," Norma added proudly.

"But I don't think you went in Union," Vincent corrected her. "Father used to live with us in Union."

"Why did Father leave Union and go to live in Kingman, Maine?" Kathleen asked innocently.

"He's the school superintendent there," Mother Millay answered and she changed the subject hurriedly.

Mother Millay still remembered with pain that dark day in Union when she had told her husband to leave and not return unless he could mend his ways. He had gambled away the money the children needed for necessities again and again. Theirs had been a good marriage in the beginning and they had been deeply in love with each other. If she could have adjusted to a gypsy, come-what-will existence with no thought of her children's future, perhaps they could have continued happily enough. But Mother Millay wanted better things for her three daughters than an uncertain nomadic existence, and the constant worry of unpaid bills in a strained atmosphere that centered around luck at the card tables. If only Henry had been able to resist the lure of gamblers' luck, how different all their lives might have been.

For the first day of school, Mother Millay planned a new dress for each of her three girls—sea green for Vincent, blue for Norma and a deep red for dark-haired Kathleen.

When the day arrived, Mother Millay had to be away on a nursing case. Vincent, as oldest daughter, was put in charge of enrolling all of them in school. Mrs. Millay made careful preparations ahead of time. She had inquired about which school to send them to, and she had their report cards from their last school.

The afternoon before, Mother Millay snatched a few hours from her own afternoon nap to give the girls a shampoo. It was a warm day so she brushed their hair dry outside in the sun until it shone.

On the first day of school, Vincent roused her two sisters early. She admonished them to eat a good breakfast—as her mother had told her to do. She supervised them carefully as they put on their new dresses. Dressed and combed, the three girls surveyed themselves in the mirror—eminently satisfied. Mother Millay was not the most skilled seamstress and her daughters had helped with the sewing. But the little mistakes in sewing did not show much, the girls decided, and they each had a new dress in cloth they had chosen themselves.

The three started for school too early. They were eager to meet their schoolmates and see the inside of the cream-colored clapboard building they had passed so many times on their way to the village. When they came to the school grounds many children had already gathered in tight little huddles in front of the building and on the playground.

The Millay girls went up the path and stood about uncertainly and a little awkwardly. They longed to approach some of the groups of girls their own age, but they did not know how. As they stood there, shy and wavering, their appearance caused a stir. Some of the girls looked at them and whispered among themselves. Vincent's sharp ears thought she could detect a titter. The boys were not as subtle.

"Yay, carrot top," shouted a red-faced boy, racing by the three girls.

"Yay, strawberry blonde," another yelled at Norma as he ran by, snapping his handkerchief in her face.

Kathleen burst into tears. Norma looked distressed. Vincent had a temper to match her hair. Her green eyes narrowed as she considered a suitable retort. She was too small and thin to fight, but she was already casting about for a way to get even with them.

"Hey, carrot top, what's your name?" the first boy asked, circling the three sisters.

"Come closer and I'll tell you," Vincent replied. She had a crafty plan. "Come closer and I'll whisper it to you," she enticed the unsuspecting boy.

He bent over toward her and she whispered her name in his ear. He turned away and shouted at the top of his lungs, "Carrots says her name is Vincent Mill—" He fell flat on his face in the gravel. Vincent had put out her foot and tripped him the moment his back was turned.

Norma and Kathleen clapped their hands. They danced around the fallen victim. "Vincent tripped him up! Vincent tripped him up!" they cried in glee.

The boy picked himself up and walked away shamefaced. A girl about Vincent's age, a bit bolder than the others, approached the group.

"Is Vincent your real name?" she asked.

"St. Vincent is my middle name. I was named after a hospital," she replied importantly.

There was an animated buzz among the girls. "She was named after a hospital," they echoed in wonder and surprise. Soon there was an admiring circle around Vincent, chattering and laughing.

"Can you swim?"

"Can you ride a bike?"

"Have you been up the mountain?"

"Have you gone fishing from the breakwater?"

"Have you been to the lake?"

They admired Vincent's dress as extravagantly and uncritically as she had. One girl touched her coppery hair, flaming in the sun.

"What long hair!" she exclaimed.

"I can sit on it," Vincent explained proudly, for her hair did hang well below her waist.

"What color is it?" she was asked.

"It's bright brown," Vincent answered. Its color was the bane of her life. People often thought Norma's hair was blond. Perhaps they might think hers a lively brown.

The school bell rang. All the children trooped inside, and the new pupils were duly enrolled. Kathleen was in the third grade, Norma in the sixth and Vincent in the eighth. They had each brought their promotion and report cards from the last school they had attended.

Mr. Wilbur, the principal, adjusted his pince-nez, as he scrutinized Vincent's cards.

"M-m-m. All A's. Very good," he said. Then he looked at Vincent. "Are you Edna St. Vincent Millay?" he asked. "Are you twelve years old? You look too young to be in the eighth grade."

Vincent was abashed. Nobody had ever before questioned her right to enter any grade. Didn't he realize she was *smart*?

At last, Mr. Wilbur reluctantly assigned Vincent to a home room in the eighth grade.

The first day of school passed quickly. In the morning, books were passed out, inkwells filled, notebooks properly labeled.

The eighth grade was taught by two teachers in rotation. The students sat in their home room while the teachers came and went. The teachers alternated in instructing the pupils in geography, arithmetic, history, civics, physiology and reading. Twice a week they took drawing and music lessons from outside teachers.

Vincent was good at her lessons—particularly reading and music. She sang in a sweet, true voice and she knew many songs her mother had taught her. She had read so much at home that the reader used by the eighth grade English class was easy for her. She had already finished all of Shakespeare's plays and most of Milton's poetry by herself. For her compositions, she wrote pages of real and imaginary adventures, and at home she still sometimes wrote poems. But Vincent liked to go to school and recite and ask the teachers questions.

School brought new friends and acquaintances. The girls were nice to her. They admired everything she did and said. Outside of school hours, there were many things to do with her new friends.

The apple orchards were ripe for picking. Every school child knew exactly where the best apples grew. Every day now, the boys and girls went on apple raids after school. Even if they were green, the apples tasted all the better for being taken by stealth.

The meadow surrounding the Millay house offered new delights in the autumn. The burdock bushes held thick clusters of blue-lavender thistles. Vincent gathered them like berries. She made baskets and boxes and mats of the prickly burdocks.

There was a horse chestnut tree across the way from their brook. Vincent often went there through the path in the woods with her sisters. The three of them sat cross legged on the ground while they broke open the pulpy, green-horned shells and carefully extracted the horse chestnuts, firm and shining new brown, each with its perfect topping of ecru shell. Working steadily, they soon had a fair-sized pile of nuts to carry home in the cotton sacks they had brought.

In October came the full glory of autumn. On the mountain, the air was like cool wine. The foliage was bright with color—red maple, the rich yellow of elm leaves and always the dark contrast of the evergreen trees. Vincent climbed the mountain many times that October. Sometimes she just sat and looked, but many times she scribbled a few words on a bit of paper she carried.

In November the trees were bare. Their skeletonlike branches were outlined grimly against the gray sky. Cold winter began to seep into the weather-beaten little house in the hollow. The basement was cold and damp. When there was a heavy rain, water rose between the planks of the floor.

Their bedrooms had no heat, although there was a banked coal fire in the living room. They heated cloth-covered bricks to keep their feet warm in bed, but by morning the rooms were bitterly cold. They scurried to the stove in the living room and dressed in the half-light with cold, stiff fingers, and then hurried through breakfast. It was a welcome relief to go off to school. There the rooms were heated and filled with sunshine by the time morning lessons began.

FOUR

Mother Millay was home between cases at Thanksgiving and the household was merry. They all sang and laughed as they dusted and swept the house from top to bottom before the holiday. The kerosene lamps were cleaned and trimmed and a roaring fire was built in the kitchen stove.

There were pumpkins and mincemeat to be made into pies. Cranberries were gathered from the bog. They bubbled merrily on the stove as Mrs. Millay stirred the deep red mixture of sugar, cranberries and water. Norma and Kathleen scraped sweet potatoes for baking, while Vincent made the stuffing for the turkey they planned to roast for dinner. Jars of mustard pickles and pickled watermelon and spiced cauliflower were lined up on the shelf. Although the Millays were poor, their Thanksgiving festivities were lavish.

"Thanksgiving is an important holiday for us," Mrs. Millay told her girls. "Our ancestors have been celebrating it for hundreds of years in this country."

"Did our ancestors celebrate the first Thanksgiving?" Kathleen asked.

"No," her mother answered. "Our family didn't land in Ipswich, Massachusetts until 1634. That means they were among the earliest settlers of this country. And our church still carries on the Pilgrim tradition."

"Are we descended from the Pilgrims?" Norma asked in awe.

"Of course we are," Vincent answered quickly. "Who else is there for us to be descended from?"

On Thanksgiving morning, Mother Millay had the girls dress in their Sunday best. After dampening down the fires, fastening the windows and latching the doors, the little family set off for the Congregational church on Elm Street which was more than a mile away. By the time they came to the white clapboard building with its tall belfry, the sermon had already begun.

The Millays caused a stir as they entered the church. Heads craned round from the red-cushioned pews to see who the latecomers were. The Reverend Evans paid no outward heed to them nor paused in his sermon, though the left corner of his mouth twitched.

This was not the first time that the Millays had trooped in late. It was a regular rite since the first Sunday they had come. Reverend Evans told himself he must speak to Mrs. Millay about it sometime—tactfully, of course. The Reverend Evans continued his sermon without a break, as he surveyed his congregation on Thanksgiving Day and recalled for them the strength and courage and piety of their ancestors who had braved the New World.

After the sermon Vincent and Norma and Kathleen went upstairs to their Sunday-school class. Vincent's teacher was Abby Evans, the minister's daughter. Abby wrote poetry, which she sometimes allowed Vincent to read. Vincent was flattered by this attention from an older girl who, in her eyes, was so poised and learned and utterly a being from another world.

Abby took Vincent aside. "Do you think you can come to church on time next Sunday?" she asked diffidently. "It's better to be a little early than late."

Vincent listened seriously to the minister's daughter and promised to come to church as punctually as she could. "We are always on time for Sunday school," she pointed out brightly. "You know I wouldn't miss it for anything."

Vincent liked to sit in the small Sunday-school room above the church where the "treasures" were kept. There was a small, authentic, early American rocker and crib which were very valuable because they were so old. The very bench they sat on must have held Pilgrim boys and girls of long ago. If Vincent tired of the Bible lesson, she could always imagine stories about the embroidered tablecloth and old parchment Bible the church owned.

Now it was Thanksgiving noon. The church bells pealed joyfully. The time had come to go home for the sumptuous Thanksgiving dinner they had had so much fun planning and preparing.

As they trudged the long mile back home, the little house in the hollow had never before beckoned so invitingly. A thin stream of smoke from the chimney signified that the fire was still going, so they all rushed into the house, sure of the warmth inside. Taking off their coats and tams, the girls rushed into the kitchen to see that all was well with the dinner. The turkey was tenderly roasting to a beautiful nut brown. The moment Mother Millay pronounced it done, Norma whisked it onto a large platter and soon it was surrounded by the yellow balls of sweet potatoes that Vincent had been preparing. Kathleen carried the colorful bowls of cranberries, pickles and side vegetables to the table. The Millays ate their Thanksgiving dinner thankfully—for the holiday had great meaning for them. Historically, it signified the arrival of their ancestors upon the shores of a new country, seeking a better way of life. Vincent vowed that each Thanksgiving she, too, would take stock and try to make their lives happier and more fruitful in this land of opportunity. Thanksgiving always ended on a note of hope, and as Mother Millay annually observed with a bright smile, "Now we can all look forward to the month of December."

With December came snow and Christmas vacation. The

fields and hills were blanketed white. Winter brush cast light shadows on the snow. Mother Millay had no work during Christmas week. At the last moment, she decided to take her daughters to Massachusetts to spend Christmas with their relatives, who had been urging them to visit ever since they left the summer before.

It was a momentous undertaking in those days to travel one hundred and sixty miles. They packed their suitcases the night before, and arose before dawn in the gray morning. Mother Millay and the three girls dressed in the dark and ate a hurried breakfast.

Taking their warmest coats and scarves and wearing tamo-shanters perched jauntily on their heads, the three girls trudged through the deep snow with their suitcases. By six o'clock they were already on board the electric trolley which followed the coast line until it traversed the length of Main Street in Rockland where the railroad terminal was.

The three girls and their mother walked the short distance to the railroad station, struggling to keep their suitcases out of the slushy snow. While Mother Millay bought their tickets, the girls explored the railroad yard and the freight office, for there was still an hour until train time.

Eventually they settled themselves in the railroad car in two of the green plush double seats, which they turned to face each other. The locomotive chugged out of the station and they were on their way. They had innumerable questions to ask about the passing towns and hamlets, the lakes and rivers they saw from the frosted windows.

It was bitterly cold that morning. Every few minutes the three girls ran to one end of the car where a potbellied iron stove gave off its grudging heat. Vincent and Norma's red curls bobbed beside Kathleen's straight dark hair as they rubbed and warmed their hands and stamped their feet. They quivered with delight when the conductor passed by with a torch and lighted the gas lamps in each car. That meant that soon they would be in a long, dark tunnel.

Now everything was pitch dark. The train went rushing through the narrow walls of the tunnel. The gaslit car jostled and shuttled from side to side. All too quickly they came to the end of the tunnel and into the harsh brightness of day.

In a few hours they reached Woolwich on the shores of the Kennebec River. This was by far the most exciting part of the journey. Here the river was a mile wide and the train was ferried across in sections.

First the locomotive tugged and chugged until each car was pushed and maneuvered into its allotted place on the ferry. Vincent and Norma and Kathleen walked through all the cars to the foremost one where they could stand on the observation platform and see everything.

The sun was bright though the water of the Kennebec was a cold, icy blue flecked with whitecaps. The wind had freshened and whipped Vincent's long hair about her face.

The ferry strained and creaked against the landing. There was a great bustling and running to and fro among the boatmen. They secured the train wheels with heavy ropes, and at last everything was ready. The ferry cast off from the wharf and moved majestically down the river in a sea of foam and spray.

When they neared the Bath shore heavy chains and ropes were thrown out to the landing, and with much clanging and creaking the ferry was secured to the posts. The passengers were shooed back into their cars while the train was reassembled on the shore. Once more the locomotive was attached to the train cars and they started southward toward Massachusetts.

The long, weary journey came to an end at last when they heard the conductor, swinging his lantern as he lurched down the aisles, calling, "Newburyport! Newburyport! New-buryport next."

"I declare, I'm just worn to a frazzle," Mrs. Millay sighed as she shepherded her lively brood down the steps to the station platform where their aunt and uncle and cousins were waiting for them.

Christmas was fun. First there was the tree to trim with silver tinsel and candles and colored ornaments. At the very top, they reverently placed the shining star of Bethlehem. While they bustled about, hiding and wrapping mysterious packages, there was a constant hum of Christmas chants and carols in the air.

On Christmas Eve, the girls hung up their stockings. In the morning they were filled with good things—red and white and green and white-striped candy canes, bags of colored agates, little toy animals and fluted Christmas candy.

The big gifts were distributed Christmas afternoon after the elaborate holiday dinner, with the entire family gathered around the Christmas tree. Heaped under it were the gaily wrapped gifts. Everybody exchanged presents with every-body else. For each of the three girls, there was a pair of skating shoes.

"Oh, Mother, shoe skates!" the three girls chorused. "We never dreamed we would have them so soon." Each hugged her treasure to her chest.

There were more practical gifts like mufflers and dresses, stockings and underwear. But shoe skates were beyond the wildest dreams of the Millay girls. The winter before, Vincent and Norma had shared a pair of skates that clamped onto their regular everyday shoes.

Everything was so wonderful and easy at their aunt's neat white house on a street with other houses. Vincent liked the wildness of their own unkempt, shingled house in Camden—weather stained and innocent of paint—in the hollow by the brook. Still, she knew they lived there because they were poor.

Vincent did not envy her aunt the gas lights, which took only the touch of a match and the turn of a knob to ignite. She preferred the softer light of candles. She did hate the kerosene lamps they sometimes used at home—the smell of the kerosene, the cleaning and trimming of the wicks, the polishing of the chimneys.

What Vincent really did envy—and so did her mother— was the all-pervading warmth in her aunt's home. There was a hot-air furnace and central heating.

Vincent luxuriated in the warmth like a cat stretching out under the stove. She lay curled up on the sofa with a book—reading to her heart's content with never a thought of an extra stick of wood on the fire. When she thought of returning to school and Camden, she wished it suddenly might be April or May.

Laden with their gifts, the Millays journeyed home. Their shining skates hung from their arms as they boarded the train. It had been the best and happiest Christmas they could remember.

The little house in the hollow—now covered with newly fallen snow—looked as picturesque as ever. No footfall marred the meadow. Norma plunged in first and cleared a crooked path with her feet just wide enough for one person to pass.

Inside it was dark and damp and cold. Exhausted, Mother Millay dropped into a chair in the dining room. Vincent sent Kathleen into the kitchen to fetch tea and water. She and Norma carried in wood for a fire in the dining room stove. It gave good heat and they could boil water for tea at the same time.

Soon there was a blazing fire. They waited and waited for Kathleen to bring the kettle of water from the kitchen.

"What do you suppose is keeping Wumpty?" Mrs. Millay asked mildly, using her pet name for Kathleen.

"That child has been gone twenty minutes," Vincent observed, assuming the role of disciplinarian of the family. "She must be up to something. You go get her, Norma."

Norma went to look. She returned convulsed with laughter.

"Mother! Vincent! Come see. I never saw anything so funny in my life," she called.

Vincent and Mother Millay crossed the room curiously. There was Kathleen skating round and round on the kitchen floor. While they were away, a water pipe had burst and flooded the kitchen; it had frozen over to a sheer expanse of ice.

"Kathleen! Stop that this minute," her mother called. "What do you think you are doing? The idea! Skating on the kitchen floor."

Vincent pointed out practically that Kathleen was doing no harm. The water on the kitchen floor had frozen over itself. She said she thought it would be a good idea if she and Norma put on *their* skates and had some fun.

Mrs. Millay laughed and admitted the justice of Vincent's observations. Norma and Vincent ran to get their skates and joined Kathleen. Now the three of them were skating together on the kitchen floor.

The lone candle threw frightening shadows on the wall. The kitchen stove sat like an angry black giant in the center. The dishes on the shelves jostled one another and rattled as first one skater went by and then another. The chairs and the table tilted at crazy angles in the dark half-light, while the girls skated round and about them and wove in and out around the kitchen.

Mrs. Millay stood laughing at them until the tears rolled down her cheeks. She returned to the dining room where she busied herself about the stove making a pot of tea for herself and hot cocoa for the girls.

Mother Millay was determined to be gay and cheerful tonight. There were dark forebodings in her mind about tomorrow when the kitchen would have to be used for cooking and not for skating. When the ice melted—as it was sure to do, either of its own accord or when a fire was built in the stove—there would be a flood of water all over the kitchen floor.

But tonight was for skating and gaiety. When the girls came upstairs for their cocoa, she sat down at the battered organ and played a rollicking tune. They sang all the jolly winter songs they knew.

FIVE

School began again. In spite of her busy days, Vincent was strangely restless. She skated with the other children on the ponds and lakes, and tramped the winter roads far and wide with them. But it did not assuage her strange longings.

Mrs. Millay began nursing a new case, and was home only for a few hours at a time to rest. Vincent missed her.

Sometimes late at night, wrapped in a blanket and perched on a window sill, Vincent watched the soft snow whirling and spewing outside. The beauty of the bare branches swaying in the wind was breath taking. But all night long it was cold. How she longed for the summer sun. She wished she were a bird and could fly away to a warmer climate. Ever since she was a tiny girl Vincent had had a special feeling of kinship and sympathy for birds. She watched them constantly, learning to know them by sight and identifying their songs. If she could have lived a carefree life like a bird—always warm and free—then life might be ideal.

It was warm in school—almost to the point of suffocation—but Vincent was beginning to find school dull. In everything except arithmetic, she was far ahead of her class.

Her best subject was English. She read avidly all the books that came her way. She liked to express her thoughts in essays and stories; her compositions were generally the best in the class.

Vincent's English class was assigned book reports, although she would have preferred to choose her own book.

There were so many wonderful things she had read. She wanted to tell everybody about the sonorous lines of Shakespeare, the beauty of Milton and Browning, the wit and warmth of Robert Louis Stevenson.

Instead, she was assigned to read James Fenimore Cooper's *The Last of the Mohicans*. It was a thick brown book, as dull and dusty on the inside as was its cover. The story moved slowly; it lacked life and color and vitality. She plowed through about one third of the book. Then she abandoned it in despair, returning to her poems and books of rousing adventure. Before the book reports were due, she had read five or six other novels.

On the day of the book reports, Vincent sat quietly in her seat in the English class. She knew she would not be called upon to give her book report until the middle of the period. She cast about in her mind for excuses. Finally, she decided to tell the truth. Then she planned to give a glowing report on the works of Edgar Allan Poe.

"Vincent, will you report on *The Last of the Mohicans* now," the teacher's sharp voice interrupted her reverie.

Vincent tossed her long red hair. A little uncertainly, she went to the front of the room and faced the class. As the others had done before her, she began in a low, quiet voice to recount the plot of *The Last of the Mohicans*. Then she paused dramatically.

"That is as far as I read," she said boldly in her piercing voice. "The book was so dull I nearly fell asleep."

Her classmates tittered. The teacher, who had not been paying close attention, looked up.

Vincent then launched into an account of some of the interesting stories she had read. She enthusiastically began describing them.

"That will do, Vincent," the teacher interrupted acidly.

"Go to your seat. You were supposed to give a book report on *The Last of the Mohicans* by James Fenimore Cooper."

"But I read six other books. They were more interesting and I want to report on them."

"Sit down and stop arguing. You're always having an argument. Now, let's see. Who's next? William, do you want to give your report on *The Connecticut Yankee* by Mark Twain."

Vincent returned to her seat abashed. She was not really perturbed about the incident until she received her report card at the end of the month.

She opened the envelope eagerly. Her report cards were generally good, but there, staring her in the face, was a C in English. She had had high marks in English all along. On a recent test, she had scored ninety-eight; C was barely passing. She trudged home in tears. Mother Millay had come home to snatch a few hours' rest. Vincent showed her the C in English on her report card and told her why her mark was so low.

Mother Millay was indignant when she heard the story. "Never you mind, Vincent," she comforted her daughter. "The first chance I get, I'll go to see the principal and straighten things out."

Mother Millay did go to see the principal. Mr. Wilbur showed no inclination to straighten things out. He stood pat on the premise that the teacher was the sole and final judge of a pupil's abilities.

"But Mr. Wilbur, Vincent had an A-plus on every composition and in every examination she took in that English class. Is it fair to the child to break her heart by giving her a C as a final mark?" Mrs. Millay pleaded.

"You seem to think your child knows more than the teacher," the principal replied acidly.

"To tell the truth, I think she does," Mrs. Millay answered with spirit. "She's a child with unusual talent. The world will hear from her one day."

"Well, I don't want to hear anything more," said Mr. Wilbur, rising from his desk and ushering Mrs. Millay into the hall. "I'm closing my office for the day. If your youngster knows more than my teachers, you needn't bother to send her back to school."

"Don't worry, I won't," Vincent's mother snapped as she followed him out into the schoolyard. There she proceeded to tell him exactly what she thought of him and his teachers and the entire school system. Mr. Wilbur tried to hush her, but Mrs. Millay went on and on until her ire was spent. The principal looked around nervously. Passers-by could hear them. He suspected that more than one householder in the neighborhood was watching the quarrel from behind raised window curtains.

"Vincent will not be back in school," Mrs. Millay announced as she finished, and flounced her skirts as she walked away. "I'll teach her myself at home. She can read the books she enjoys and develop her talents. Someday you will regret this, Mr. Wilbur, I warn you."

Vincent's days at home were long and lonely. She saw Norma and Kathleen off to school every morning and longed to be going, too.

When her mother came home in the afternoon, they built a roaring fire and drank hot tea. Then they reviewed the lessons which Vincent had studied by herself.

During the rare intervals when Mrs. Millay was home for a few days at a time between cases, they had a wonderful time together. It was almost as much fun as going to school. They read poetry aloud. Vincent learned about far-off places. They studied music—singing and playing wonderful, thrilling songs.

Mrs. Millay was an accomplished pianist, and she began

teaching Vincent to play the battered old organ which stood in their parlor. Vincent, who had an ear for music, was soon picking out tunes. Before long, she was composing little songs of her own to the poems she wrote.

These interludes never lasted very long, for Mrs. Millay was always called away on a new case.

Vincent spent many dreary winter days in the public library, which consisted of one stuffy room on the second floor of a red brick business block on Main Street. The books were tightly locked behind glass-faced cupboards. Vincent always felt an intruder before the eagle-eyed librarian who looked askance at the fragile, red-haired girl of twelve who was not at school with the other children. Still, the library was warm and Vincent could study there until it was time to rush home to start the fire in the stove for her mother's homecoming.

Vincent advanced rapidly in her studies.

"At the rate you are going, Sefe," Mrs. Millay said to her, using her pet name which was a contraction of Josephus, "you will soon be finishing the eighth grade."

Vincent shrugged her shoulders.

"What difference does it make if I finish the eighth grade," she asked, "if I don't go to school?"

Vincent, with the wisdom of twelve years, felt that anyone who did not go to school was a freak. She might be learning twice as much at home, but she was not one of the crowd. She never could be unless she, too, went to school.

On Washington's birthday—February 22—she would be thirteen years old. She felt herself in disgrace in the eyes of the world. What a failure her life was—even before she had become thirteen.

"Little princesses don't go to school," Mrs. Millay told her.

"I'm not a little princess," Vincent pointed out practically. "Norma and Kathleen go to school."

"You can be a princess in spirit," her mother suggested. "And you'll know your sisters' friends. You can play with them."

Vincent nodded mournfully. She could not stoop to pick up the crumbs of her two younger sisters' school life. She could not be friends with their friends, she was too proud and they were too young.

"If you finish the eighth grade and study through the summer, perhaps you can skip the ninth grade," Mrs. Millay proposed. "Then you won't have to go back to the Elm Street school at all."

It was a point of honor with Mrs. Millay not to send Vincent back to Mr. Wilbur's school. Moreover, there was a real doubt in her mind that Vincent would be allowed to re-enter even if she wanted to.

Mrs. Millay was distraught at her daughter's unhappiness and tried to distract her. Instead of having Vincent go home from the library to start the stove fires in their cheerless house, she took her to the simple little restaurant, known as the Two by Twice Lunchroom, for hot chocolate and cookies. Vincent now came to call for her mother at the Tufts's home, which was a large white mansion near the mall. Mrs. Tufts was her mother's patient.

The first time Vincent rang the bell—a slight figure in a long coat and lavender and white stocking cap—the door opened quietly. Vincent stood in the hall viewing with awe the great mirror and highly polished mahogany furniture. Through the wide doors she caught a glimpse of shining hardwood floors, richly upholstered damask chairs and luxuriously thick rugs.

"Come right in, dear," a soft voice said. "Your mother will be down in a moment. And next time, please don't ring the bell. Just come in and sit quietly."

Vincent nodded silently and waited until her mother appeared.

Every day Vincent came to the Tufts's home for her mother. As she grew more accustomed to its spacious grandeur, she ventured to peep through the door into the front parlor. There in solitary splendor stood a grand piano. Vincent was fascinated by it. She tiptoed in softly. She walked around it once. Then she sat down tentatively.

She touched one key and was in ecstasy. The note she struck was pure and rich. She trilled the keys experimentally and soon forgot her surroundings. The unbidden guest sat down and forcefully played one of her own compositions. Her long stocking cap bobbed over one shoulder as she bent over the keyboard. She finished her spirited song with a flourish.

"Bravo! Bravo!" a male voice called and there was the sound of mock applause.

Vincent whirled around, surprised and startled.

Behind the man stood her mother, reproach in her gray eyes reluctantly mingled with pride.

"Vincent, how could you!" Mrs. Millay exclaimed. "The very idea! Coming into Mrs. Tufts's house and sitting down at the piano."

"Don't scold her," Mr. Tufts interceded. "Where did you learn to play that tune?"

Vincent hung her head. "I made it up myself," she said softly.

Mr. Tufts grew excited. "Are you sure you made it up yourself? Didn't you hear it anywhere?"

"No, I made it up myself on the organ at home," Vincent replied.

"Is that true, Mrs. Millay?" Mr. Tufts asked.

"My daughters are very truthful," Mrs. Millay answered

with quiet dignity, her small bobbed head shaking with indignation.

Mr. Tufts took both her tiny, work-worn hands in his. "She is a wonder!" he exclaimed. "She is a wonder! I want to teach her myself. That such a child plays like this is a wonder."

Mrs. Millay dropped her eyes. "You know what I earn here a week," she reminded him. "I'll try to find the money. . . ."

"Don't let the money worry you, Mrs. Millay," the lank music teacher interrupted. "I consider it a great privilege to teach this girl. Mark my words, she is a wonder."

Vincent became John Tufts's most favored pupil. His house was her second home. She often practiced for hours there without pause. No more than one hour a day was required of the average student, but Vincent's ambition now was to be a concert pianist when she grew up.

She could see herself clearly now—grown older and already a famous concert pianist. Her hair would be darker, a true chestnut brown. She would pile it high on her head and lace it with gold ribbons. Her dress would be made of iridescent watered silk green taffeta, long and *bouffant*. It would rustle slightly as she walked on stage. Her shoes would be dainty and gold with the highest heels imaginable. Or, glory of glories, her dress could be scarlet if her hair were truly brown.

Wearing the bright red dress of her dreams, Vincent would bow to the audience. Then she would play—perhaps something by Beethoven or Mozart—occasionally a composition of her own. There would be applause and applause, which she would acknowledge gracefully. Sometimes she would play an encore; sometimes she would not, no matter how much they applauded.

These dreams raced busily through her head all the time

she was practicing her scales. Hers would be a wonderful life when she was grown up and famous. She did not mind too much now being barred from school. Everybody knew that concert pianists—like princesses—were taught by private tutors.

SIX

Early in February Vincent sat alone at the window in the winter dusk idly contemplating her thirteenth birthday, which fell on the twenty-second of that month. She wondered whether her presents would be nice this year. She supposed there would be a party and a birthday cake with white icing and multicolored candy sprinkled on it—thirteen pink candles in pink holders and an extra one in the middle to grow on. At the party there would be only her mother, Norma and Kathleen. Vincent had nobody to invite. For a moment, she had a pang of regret that she no longer went to school with the other girls and boys. If she studied during the summer, she could skip the ninth grade and enter high school next September. Then she would have friends her own age and she could still be a concert pianist when she grew up. It was hard to be almost thirteen and not have one real chum.

Vincent started laying the supper plates on the table while waiting for Norma and Kathleen to return from school. Supper in the Millay household was rarely a sumptuous affair. Vincent planned the meals now and whatever struck her fancy at the moment was quickly bought or sent for. Rarely was there a reserve of preserved food in the house as there was in most well-stocked Maine larders. With twelve-year-old Vincent in charge of the meals, the Millay girls literally ate from hand to mouth.

Vincent laid aside for her mother the letter that had come

from Kingman, Maine, in the afternoon mail. It was from Henry, her father, she knew, and she wondered what news it would bring. She still remembered that day in Union when her mother had sent him away. Her father had gone around to the back and across the bog and then disappeared. Now there was no bitterness or rancor between her mother and father—just an utter weariness on Mrs. Millay's part with the gambling fever that afflicted him.

When Mrs. Millay returned home in the late afternoon, she found the letter waiting for her on the table. She opened it quickly, and a check fluttered out. It was for twenty dollars!

After the first cry of pleasure and surprise, Mrs. Millay's lips tightened. How like Henry! They could not depend on him for day to day sustenance. That she had learned with tears and sorrow. Now suddenly there was a large sum (for twenty dollars could buy much more then) "to buy something special for the girls." It was Henry's way of saying that luck had been with him at the card tables. Though he was the best poker player in town, he was not always lucky.

Mrs. Millay sighed. She put away the check under a stack of plates for safekeeping. She had been saving every spare dollar for a piano. Some days the stoves burned so much coal she could scarcely make ends meet. Now they could buy the piano in time for Vincent's birthday and have a little over for a birthday party and cake.

Mother Millay was determined to give her daughters all the advantages and opportunities that she herself had missed. Her mother had died when she was young and the five children of the family had been scattered among various relatives. As a youngster, she had written verses and had wanted to become a concert pianist, too. It had had to remain a dream. Instead, she had met Henry Millay at a grange meeting where she was playing the piano for the dancing. They had

fallen madly in love and married. Now she was alone, struggling to feed and clothe their three daughters. If only Henry
had lavished all the subtleties of his charm and the keen-
ness of his fine mathematical mind on his position as school
superintendent instead of on games of chance. . . .

Now Vincent could have a piano and practice as many
hours a day as she wished. Perhaps she would grow up to
be a famous pianist or writer or actress. The child had so
many talents, sometimes it frightened her. She must help her
in every way she could.

The day before Vincent's birthday was a cold, clear winter
day. The snow lay shining and bright on the meadow. Vincent stirred beneath the warmth of the bedclothes, blinking
her eyes in the strong sun. Norma and Kathleen would be
trudging off to school now, but she had other things to do.

Today was the day the piano was coming. She must decide where it was to stand and how it was to be placed. She
must not under any circumstances leave the house before the
men came to deliver it. Mother had left everything up to her.
She must prove herself dependable.

Were those sleigh bells she heard? In a second Vincent
had leaped out of bed and was peering anxiously out of the
window. No, the sleigh was driving straight past the crest
of the hill and did not turn into the hollow. It could not
possibly be the one bringing the piano.

Vincent stood in a pool of sunlight and stretched luxuriously. Oh, it was good to be alive on a day like this! The sun
warmed her through and through. She had not been so comfortable for months—inside or out. Her thirteenth birthday
would bring a good year, she knew. She could feel it in the
very marrow of her bones.

She slipped into her clothes and brought back to the sunny
spot by the window a cup of cocoa warmed over from the
night before.

How she wished they would hurry! It was already almost nine o'clock in the morning. All good, honest Maine working people had started their labors two hours ago. Where were those men?

The piano itself would be a surprise. Mother and Mr. Tufts had selected it. Mr. Tufts had heard of several good secondhand pianos to be bought in the county. He and Mrs. Millay had tested and touched and knocked each one for soundness and fidelity of tone. Finally they chose the one they considered the best.

Vincent had not suspected the reason her mother had seemed so strangely busy and preoccupied the past few weeks. Only yesterday her mother had told her that the piano was to be delivered this morning. Vincent's happiness was boundless when she heard the news.

A piano of her own! Now she could practice as much as she liked, choosing her own hours. Before, she had always had to plan to use Mr. Tufts's piano when he would not need it for his pupils or for himself.

Vincent knew there had been many times when her teacher had wanted to play. But he had sacrificed the piano to her, saying, "You are young, child. You have a gift for the world. But you must work and work and work. There is no easy way."

With a piano of her own, she could lose herself in the music, playing on and on with no thought of Mr. Tufts's piano students due to come in twenty minutes or half an hour.

When she was a famous concert pianist, she would go from great city to great city giving concerts. Even if she traveled to the capitals of far-off Europe, her own piano would go with her. All great musicians toured thus, she had read.

While she was dreaming of fame and success, a large

sleigh glided into the hollow. The tinkle of sleigh bells reached her ears as in a dream. With a start, Vincent realized that the piano had arrived.

She ran downstairs to answer the sharp rap on the door. A man in a sheepskin-lined coat and cap with ear muffs stood there. He held an important-looking paper in his hands.

"Piano for Vincent Millay?" he announced in his deep voice.

"Yes, I am Vincent Millay," she answered eagerly.

"Don't fool me, little girl. You tryin' to be a boy?"

"But I am Vincent Millay—*Edna* Vincent Millay—and the piano is for me."

"Well, if you say so . . ." the man paused doubtfully and called his helper.

They both looked at her thoughtfully, then shook their heads and turned back to the sleigh without another word.

Vincent was in despair. They were going to drive the sleigh away with the piano, and with it would go her glittering career. Her dream world toppled. Under its deceptive sunniness, the day was cold. She could feel the cold now, knifing its way into her bones.

But wait! The men were not driving away. They were removing the canvas and innumerable blankets in which the piano was wrapped. They were urging the horse nearer to the steps of the house.

Vincent ran down the steps to the sleigh. The piano was a beauty—small and upright, of glowing cherry wood, beautifully burled and polished. Vincent fell in love with it at once. She could scarcely contain herself as she danced round and about it.

The two men looked at her with quizzical tolerance. They had never seen a little girl so excited at the sight of a piece of furniture.

At last the piano stood across one corner of the living

room. The beautiful grain of the wood shone from top to bottom. Vincent promised herself she would dust and polish it faithfully every day to keep it always as beautiful as it was now.

One of the men went back to the sleigh to get the matching bench that came with the piano. It, too, was small and oblong but gracefully proportioned with slim, straight legs.

"There, young lady, now you have your piano," the older of the two men exclaimed heartily. "How about giving us a tune?"

Vincent slipped quietly onto the bench and started playing. The tone was rich and true. Vincent was soon lost in a sea of sound.

The men listened—first in amusement, then in slight awe. Vincent had completely forgotten they were there.

In time, they trudged heavily downstairs to their sleigh and neighing horse. The younger remarked rather grumpily, "She might have at least offered us a cup of hot coffee. Some people's children!"

Vincent's birthday was also George Washington's birthday, so it was a school holiday. And to add to their delight, Mother Millay had arranged to be home for a good part of the day, too.

In the morning Vincent and Norma and Kathleen went for a long walk. They skirted the mountain, its summit now hidden in lead-heavy clouds. They took the back road through the winding woods toward Lake Megunticook. It was a long, peace-filled walk. On the way back it began to snow.

The snow fell softly on the blanketed earth, swirling and blowing in fitful starts. Kathleen skipped about like a joyful kitten. She gathered the new-fallen snow in soft puffs that immediately disappeared in her mittened hands.

Vincent took Norma aside to share a grown-up thought with her. "Look quick over there by the tree branch where the snow is coming out in spurts. Doesn't it look as if someone is spitting out snow?"

"Yes, it does," Norma agreed heartily.

"Isn't the world a beautiful place!" Vincent called, capering around Kathleen.

"It is, it is!" Norma cried as she joined her.

Little Kathleen looked from one sister to the other in bewilderment. She joined in the fun even though she was a bit too young to understand why they were so excited. Breathless and rosy cheeked, they burst into the house where Mother Millay was waiting for them.

The kitchen was warm and inviting. Every corner was scrupulously clean.

"Girls, girls, where have you been?" she asked. "Dinner is ready and all we have to do is set the table."

"Oh, Mother, let me set the table," Kathleen begged. "I know how, I think. Knife and spoon on the right hand side of the plate, water glass above. . . ."

"All but two of the water glasses are broken," interrupted Norma. "We were singing Vincent's song and all of them slipped out of the dishpan onto the floor."

"Never mind the water glasses," Mother Millay said kindly. "Today is Vincent's birthday and we mustn't spoil it by thinking of what we don't have."

"Mother, won't it be wonderful when we're rich some day?" Vincent put in. "We won't ever worry about water glasses. We'll have beautiful silver serving plates for meat and vegetables. There'll be lovely white damask tablecloths and flowers and tall white candles. . . ."

"Child, child! How you go on!" Mother Millay exclaimed laughing. "I hope you do get all you want sometime. But in the meantime, do you think you can come down to earth long enough to eat clam chowder and cherry pie from a red and white checked tablecloth."

Kathleen sat down contentedly beside Norma. Mother Millay brought the freshly baked cherry pie to the table. She ladled generous portions of the thick, milky clam chowder into the chipped soup plates. At each place was a little hatchet made of silver paper with a red paper handle, and a bowl of polished apples sat in the middle of the table.

"It's the best birthday dinner I ever had," Vincent said happily as she spooned up the clam chowder. "Everything matches in red and white. The hatchets make me feel as if I'm celebrating right along with little George Washington. I'd like to be famous, too, when I grow up."

"You do have distinguished ancestors, children," Mrs. Millay said. "Our people have been in this country since long before the American Revolution. On my side of the family, the Emerys . . ."

"But your maiden name was Buzzel—Cora Lounella Buzzell," interrupted Norma.

"My mother was an Emery," Mrs. Millay continued proudly. "The Emerys were a very old Belfast family. They came originally from Normandy in France. Gilbert d'Amory was a Norman baron who accompanied William the Conqueror to England. After that the name became Emery. Our family landed in Ipswich, Massachusetts, in 1634 and 1635. . . ."

"That's near Newburyport," Vincent exclaimed.

"Yes, Ipswich is very near Newburyport," Mother Millay agreed.

"Didn't we go to the cemetery there once?" Norma asked. "It seems to me we did."

"Yes, we all went to the graves of our ancestors one Memorial Day," Mrs. Millay answered. "And the father of our earliest American ancestor lies buried at Romsey Hants in England. His name was John Emery. Someday we'll all go to England to the county of Hampshire and visit his grave, too."

Vincent's imagination was easily kindled by the glories of the past and inflamed by the fame of the future. Her eyes blazed their darkest green as she exclaimed, "You just wait till we're rich. We'll go to Romsey Hants in England and all over the world—Paris, China, India, everywhere."

With that, Vincent swept up the steps to the living room, her long red hair flowing behind her like a mantilla. The rest of the family followed eagerly.

Vincent seated herself at the new piano and began playing "The Scarf Dance." The music filled the small, drab room tempestuously. Suddenly Vincent swung into the opera *Aïda*. Norma sprang to her side to sing the soprano roles. Kathleen ran to the piano to sing the choruses. Mother Millay was conductor and impresario. If all went well, they usually managed to gallop through the score in an hour or so.

Aïda, sung and played with gusto, echoed and re-echoed until the walls of the little house shook. When the last ringing note was finished, the twilight was gathering.

It was time for tea and the lighting of the birthday candles. Kathleen proudly boiled the water on the potbellied stove in the living room. Norma prepared the tea things. Mrs. Millay fetched the birthday cake from its secret hiding place.

One by one the fourteen candles—one for each year and one to grow on—were lighted. The family gathered around the table. Vincent looked pensively at the high, round cake iced with white frosting and sprinkled with birthday candy in many colors. Each pink candle burned with a small, valiant flame, struggling against the sudden cold drafts that came and went in the room.

Mother Millay brought a woolen shawl. She put it across Vincent's shoulders, urging her gently, "Come now, Vincent, make your birthday wish."

Vincent thought intently a few moments; then she made her birthday wish. A thirteenth birthday was a momentous occasion. It could be a lucky year—oh! so lucky!—or it could be the unluckiest one in the world.

Vincent was surprised at her silent wish. She had never expected to wish that, but it was too late to change now.

She blew as hard as she could. All the candles were extinguished by one hard puff and they sat in the room in darkness.

"Vincent got her wish! Vincent got her wish!" Kathleen cried in delight, breaking the silence.

"What did you wish?" Norma asked. "You can tell now because you're going to get your wish anyway."

"I wished I could go to school like all the other girls do," Vincent burst out.

"Oh, Vincent, what did you wish that for?" exclaimed Norma. "You could have wished for something good."

"That's a very good wish," Mrs. Millay said firmly. "It shows Vincent has character. I'm real proud of you, Sefe." It was a mark of genuine affection when Mother Millay addressed Vincent as Sefe.

"You can go back to school next fall—and not to grammar school, either," Mother Millay continued. "You're smart enough to skip a grade and go right into high school. Would you like to do that, Sefe?"

"Oh, yes, I'd rather do that than anything else in the world," answered Vincent. "I'd be the youngest girl in high school. Then nobody could say I wasn't smart—not even the teacher."

SEVEN

High school was a revelation to Vincent. Everybody was new in the freshman class so nobody knew one another well enough to make her feel an outsider. Some of the boys and girls came from other towns; the rest had graduated from the various grammar schools scattered throughout Camden.

There were twice as many boys as girls, Vincent noticed with a certain amount of interest, and she decided the girls looked jolly. Though most of them were a year or two older than she, Vincent thought they could be friends. She was the youngest and the smallest and certainly the thinnest girl in the freshman class.

High school students were no longer treated as children. The teachers now addressed Vincent as "Miss Millay." All the boys were called by their surnames. No first name. No mister. Just "Gamage, Pease, Blood, Pendleton."

It gave Vincent a sense of bustling importance to troop around from class to class. The new high school building was so clean and modern. There would even be electric lights in the assembly hall—the only room not yet completed in time for the opening of school.

Vincent felt such strong emotion about attending high school at last that it could not be contained within herself. One night at home she plied her pencil heavily as she wrote:

THE NEWEST FRESHMAN

The newest freshman dropped into her seat and began to arrange her books. First came history. That was

the largest. Then algebra, Latin, English, all with the
bindings inward. Must she look up now? No. English,
Latin, algebra, history, all with the bindings outward.
There was nothing else to do. She must look up. She
raised her eyes and glanced around the room.

There was nothing unusual about the room. A floor,
four walls and a ceiling. She had seen them before. It
would be hard; she was prepared for that: Sitting into
the small hours of the night with an algebra book in her
lap and a *Beginner's Latin* at her elbow and a map of
Mars on the table before her. She wondered if she were
the only one that would have to do that. Perhaps not.

Once more she glanced around the room, this time at
the other scholars. She should like them all. She knew
some of them, and to her own knowledge they had, at
some time, attended the grammar school.

She would like all the lessons. She loved Latin already, algebra she liked, history she had no idea of.

Suddenly, all went to their seats. She did not know
why. She had heard no bell ring. But in some way unknown to her, they knew it was time to be seated. It
might be wireless telegraphy. It was Greek to her.

How strange it seemed to be a part of a real high
school. She had never been so honored. She felt grateful to the whole school for allowing her to be an in-
habitant of the Elysian Field, of which she had no chart.

The newest freshman stood greatly in awe of all the
members of her own class as well as of the other classes.
They, one and all, could tell the product of X and A;
she could not. The sophomores, individually, collec-
tively and without exception, had forgotten when they
were freshmen. The juniors had better memories. The
seniors; oh, well! They were not so inspiring after all,

she thought, as she watched one of the "favored few,"
at the board, spell perpendicular with two *i*'s.

A week passed on, and she had settled down to the
declension of *hasta* and the conjugation of *amo* without a tremor. Indeed, she felt rather strange one morning when the twenty-ninth example was assigned to
Miss Millay and she was told to "put it on the board."
But what of it?

She got there as quietly as the others and drifted in
between two of her strangest companions. Then she
commenced. It went along more smoothly than she had
any hope of, and she backed into her seat, eying it ap-
provingly. She was glad it was not the first; it was a
happy medium, and she liked that just now.

Her name was called again that day, this time to recite. She did remarkably well, considering that she
could not keep her thoughts from a book she had just
been reading, a criticism of Darwin's theory, and she
felt as if someone had turned on an electric battery in
the room. There might be one in the laboratory. She
walked home on air that day.

Next came an examination in algebra. That would be
the hardest of all, she thought. But she watched the
number of examples to be done diminish as the number
of examples done increased, with pardonable pride.

Sixth, seventh, eighth, ninth—the tenth she could not
do. She looked around at the bare walls for inspiration.
There was none. Oh, for an algebra and the right to
use it! She read it again. Perhaps she had copied it down
wrong. No; she compared the figures, one by one. They
were all right. It was no use. She could not do it. She
sighed and folded the paper with a last reproving glance
at the stubborn tenth. She wrote her name quickly and
delivered it into the hands of a businesslike personage,

out of harm's way. Then she went to her seat, drew out her algebra book and looked it up. There was the rule staring at her from the page in mocking letters. The square of the difference of two quantities is equal to the square of the first, minus twice the product of the two, plus the square of the second. She would never fail that again.

It was well past midnight when Vincent finished the composition. She folded it carefully lengthwise as she had been instructed to do. Placing the fold at the left, she wrote her name in the upper corner and beneath it put English IV. Then came the date.

Vincent wondered if the teacher would know why she was the "newest" freshman. Mrs. Millay had had a long talk with the high school principal Mr. Mitchell during the summer. Mr. Mitchell had agreed to take Vincent into the freshman class on trial. If she could keep up with the work and received passing marks, she could stay. Vincent vowed to study hard. Failure would be ignominious.

Vincent, for all that she had been intrigued by the romantic sound of algebra, soon discovered that it was only another name for a more disagreeable form of arithmetic. She had always found figures impossible. Figures plus the letters x, y and z with their mysterious function left her in a complete state of bewilderment.

In a few weeks, the hustle and bustle and excitement of going to high school wore off. Algebra became Vincent's bugaboo. Though she was the star pupil in Latin and English, she dreaded going to algebra class. The homework was a nightmare. The examinations were worse, for the problems became progressively harder and more complicated.

She knew she would have to leave high school if she failed in algebra. She wondered whether she ought to con-

centrate only on being a concert pianist and resign volun-
tarily before the report cards came due.

In the meantime, she managed to make many friends. She
was immediately popular with the girls in the freshman class.
There were the three Alices, Ethel, Stella, Florence, Vivian,
Maud, Marion, Mary and Nina. Since they were all so very
nice to her, she did not know who she wanted for her closest
chum. She liked them all.

Vincent was happy in her new-found companionship.
She had already visited most of the girls for the after-school
hours and supper. They, in turn, came to the little house in
the hollow. Vincent soon had an amicable arrangement with
Stella, a healthy, bouncing girl with bright brown eyes. Stella
helped Vincent with algebra while Vincent prepared the
homework in Latin.

In addition to her other talents, Stella could cook potato
soup. In the eyes of the Millay girls, this made her a supreme
cook. Stella was a frequent guest as the bleak Maine winter
set in. Vincent entertained her for hours by playing "The
Scarf Dance" and all the other pieces she learned in her piano
studies. Stella was a willing enough audience of one.

When the homework and music were over, Vincent would
begin to plan the supper. If there were potatoes and a piece
of pork in the house, Stella would concoct her famous potato
soup. If there was nothing for a hot supper, Vincent would
send Norma and Kathleen downtown for pie and milk. Once
they were sent to the bakery for a date pie. Vincent and Stella
were still busy comparing their homework in the sitting
room. Norma and Kathleen were in the kitchen where they
were arguing. The argument led to a quarrel. When Vincent
and Stella arrived to calm them, Kathleen had put the date
pie on the floor and was jumping up and down on it with
both feet. They ate supper that night at Stella's home.

The little house in the hollow was now always full of

girls—Vincent's friends, Norma's, Kathleen's. Though it was bitterly cold there during the winter, Vincent's chums liked to sleep there overnight. There were no adults about to tell them what they ought or ought not to do. They snuggled close to the stove in the living room even though that meant sleeping on the floor. They covered themselves with every blanket and quilt they could lay their hands on and often with the heavy portieres that hung at the windows. Norma and Kathleen were required to sleep in their bedroom and in beds. On that point Vincent was adamant. Sleeping on the floor beside the stove was not for younger sisters.

Vincent's ideas about housekeeping were original, too. When every dish in the house had been used, and the milk bottles stood on the kitchen floor in rows like tin soldiers in battle formation, Vincent would strike up her song "Down Where the Dishmop River Flows." Norma and Kathleen would chime in with the verses Vincent had composed. Their childish trebles urged the visiting girls on. As they all washed dishes furiously, they sang the chorus:

"There are pots and pans and kettles galore.
When I think I'm all done there's always some more.
For here's a dozen and there's a score.
I'm the Queen of the Dishpans—hooray!"

The rusting iron sink overflowed with peaked mounds of soap suds, and the dishes and bottles and silverware sloshed around in the steaming water. Vincent busily fetched boiling hot water from the kettle on the stove. She supervised the girls in their tasks, praising one and chiding another and encouraging them in their work with song and doggerel.

"Look, Vincent, I've washed twenty-two milk bottles," Stella exclaimed in pride as she surveyed the scrupulously scrubbed glass glistening from its last rinsing.

"And I've wiped all the forks and spoons and knives and seventeen plates," put in little Kathleen as she worked industriously in another corner of the kitchen. Because Kathleen was the youngest, the lightest tasks were assigned to her.

At the irregular intervals when they cleaned the house or washed the dishes, Vincent always made a game of it. The other girls actually liked washing dishes and scrubbing pots at the Millays'.

"You wouldn't do so much work at home," the mothers grumbled to their daughters, "but you're only too glad to go over to the Millays and work there."

"Oh, Mother, we have fun," was the invariable reply. "Besides, Vincent helps us with our Latin. We could never get through those awful declensions and conjugations by ourselves."

"I notice you help her do her algebra, too, young lady," a mother would sniff.

Though Vincent was popular with the girls, the teachers had mixed feelings about her. The youngest and smallest in her class, Vincent was also the most talkative. Except for algebra, her studies came easily to her. Though she soon had a reputation among the teachers of being smart as a whip, they found her troublesome because she was so argumentative.

Was there a moot point on some obscure event in ancient Greek history? Vincent's hand was immediately raised to dispute the teacher's interpretation. Sometimes she really wanted to know something. At other times, the teachers were positive it was merely to delay a quiz or question period for the other pupils.

"Miss Millay, that will do. We'll have no more arguments on the subject," the teacher would say bluntly in order to shut off the torrent of words with which she used to confound them.

The next moment her hand would be waving again. She was off on another subject—nothing daunted.

As the ringleader among the girls, Vincent was a natural target for the boys. At the class meetings she was always bubbling over with suggestions. Whenever Vincent rose to speak, all the boys began talking at once in loud voices. They created such a din that she could not be heard above it. They stamped their feet on the floor to show their disapproval of whatever she might be proposing.

This did not in the least deter Vincent. She was always ready with a new idea, though sometimes she wished the atmosphere was not so rife with catcalls whenever she spoke.

At the Friday night socials, Vincent played musical chairs and Tucker with the others. They all danced the Virginia reel together. Although Vincent and Stella knew how to waltz, nobody else in their class did, and there was no social dancing.

After the social was over none of the boys offered to walk home with Vincent, as they sometimes did with the other girls. She tossed her head, pretending she didn't care, though deep down she really did. Of course, no boy was as smart as she was and she knew it. Still, she would have liked to have a boy—nobody in particular—or maybe two or three to walk home with her after the Friday evening socials.

Vincent felt that all her new friendships and interests were tentative until her school marks should prove her right to continue high school. She waited eagerly for the day of the report cards, though she was frightened, too.

"Well, I might just as well face it. At least now I'll know," she said philosophically to calm herself as she took the square white card on which her marks were recorded. She peeped at it fearfully with half-shut eyes. Spelling, *A*. Algebra, *B*. Her heart jumped for joy. *B* was a passing mark; she had not failed. She wondered if Mr. Mitchell had noticed how hard she had tried. She skimmed over the rest of the report card. History, *A*. Drawing, *A*. How sweet of Miss Cleveland to give her an *A* in drawing. Latin, *A*. She had expected that. She was just about the best student in the class. English, *A*.

She could stay in high school. She would!

Now that Vincent's position in high school was secure, she had many things to do. She still practiced long hours each day, for her amibition to become a famous concert pianist had not slackened.

At school she belonged to the Latin Club and she was a forward on the basketball team. She was also a member of Genethod—a club organized by the Congregational church for its younger members. Outside of school hours, there was the Sunday Afternoon Tea Club, devoted to walks, and the Huckleberry Finners, a reading circle of girls so named because the first book they read together was *Huckleberry Finn*.

Best of all, Vincent, together with Vivian Dodge, the other red-haired girl in the freshman class, was appointed to the editorial board of the high school magazine—*The Megunticook*. When Vincent's composition, "The Newest Freshman" was printed in *The Megunticook*, Mother Millay was happy and proud. Vincent took this triumph in her stride. She wanted to have her poems published and she wanted to distinguish herself outside of the hard little fishing town of Camden. Vincent wanted to be done with being "the newest freshman" and be known in the wide world.

She began sending her poetry to *St. Nicholas*, the children's literary magazine, for possible use in the St. Nicholas League, a special section consisting wholly of contributions submitted by its young readers.

EIGHT

Vincent waited eagerly for the *St. Nicholas* magazine. She rushed home at noon from school to ransack the mailbox, and ran to meet the postman on his afternoon rounds, red hair flying and thin face strained toward him.

"Anything for me, Mr. Ames, anything for me?" she shrilled at the stooped figure plodding down the street.

"You expecting a letter from your sweetie?" Mr. Ames asked, his old face breaking into a thousand wrinkles as he grinned from ear to ear.

"No, no!" Vincent protested vigorously, blushing as she denied it. "I'm waiting for my magazine."

"You must be following the serial story. Love story, too, I bet. What foolishness the young ones go in for nowadays," Mr. Ames observed disapprovingly.

"I am not," Vincent denied. "I am waiting for something —*important*."

The postman was not impressed.

One sunny day the magazine did come. Vincent snatched it from the postman's outstretched hand just as he was about to put it in their mailbox. In furious haste she tore off the wrappings.

She was now a member in good standing of the St. Nicholas League. She had received her certificate and badge and—together with many other children from every state of the union and from as far away as Hawaii—she mailed an original poem to the League almost every month on the assigned subject. The best poems were printed in the St. Nicholas League section in the back of the magazine. Vincent's name had been on the Roll of Honor twice. Once it was in the list of those poems which showed promise. The second time it was in the "List of those whose work would have been used had space permitted."

Vincent, of course, turned first to the St. Nicholas League section in the back of the magazine. Her name was not on the Roll of Honor this month. Disappointed, she leafed idly through the pages where the League contributions were printed.

She stopped, for she could not believe her eyes. Was it true? She looked again. Yes, it seemed real enough. There at the top of the page was the date, October, 1906. She knew that was so. Below it at the top of the page was a photograph. There, printed in the second column on the right, was her poem—along with stories and poems and photographs by children from all over the world.

First came the title—"Forest Trees." Then came her name —by Vincent Millay (Age 14). Vincent thought she had never seen anything so beautiful in all her life. Her name looked so strange, yet so elegant, in print. The letters in her first name marched across the page in orderly fashion led by the dashing *V*. The *y* of Millay ended with a flourish. It was some time before she turned to the poem itself, so rapt was she in contemplating the effect of her name in print.

She knew every word in the poem by heart. She had said it over to herself many times in the past months. She skimmed over the lines now. Every word was perfect.

Monarchs of long-forgotten realms, ye stand;
    Majestic, grand;
Unscarred by Time's destructive hand.
Enthroned on dais on velvet moss, inset
With royal purple of the violet;
    And crowned with mistletoe.

How many ages o'er your heads have flown,
　　To you is known—
To you, ye forest-founders of the past, alone.
No other eyes may scan the breadth of years,
Each with its share of peace, and joy, and tears;
　　Of happiness and woe.

Around you all is change—where now is land
Swift vessels plowed to foam the seething main;
Kingdoms have risen, and the fire fiend's hand
Has crushed them to their mother earth again;
And through it all ye stand, and still will stand
Till ages yet to come have owned your reign.

The poem seemed so wonderful and impressive in print. It was a thing apart now—just as if she had never written it herself.

Did I really write this? she mused in wonder. It is so good.

Supper was a festive occasion that evening in the Millay household. Vincent went downtown to do the shopping herself and bought all their favorite foods. She concocted a shrimp wiggle dish and there was pecan pie for dessert. They ate in the dining room with autumn leaves and candles on the table. At each place Vincent put a copy of her poem. After supper, she recited it to her two sisters in a serious and impressive voice. She topped off the evening by serving each of them a tiny glass of dandelion wine. They made faces as they bravely sipped it, for it was of last year's vintage and overstrong and bitter by now. They all went to bed bewildered and drowsy from Vincent's first taste of fame.

But her big triumph would be the next day. What a grand beginning for her sophomore year in high school! How impressed her schoolmates would be when they saw her poem in a real magazine published in faraway New York.

As she started for school the next morning, Vincent carefully put the magazine on top of her textbooks. It was a dull, gray day. The only spot of color on the landscape was the tiny figure of the young girl in her bright green coat and lavender stocking cap. The waters of the brook rushed by frostily.

But it was spring in Vincent's heart as she hurried down Washington Street to the schoolhouse. She hugged the magazine closely to her, feeling warmed by it.

Every few moments she stopped to open the magazine and peer intently at her poem. It was still there as real as life. She noticed another poem on the same page as hers but in the first column. It was "The Forest" by E. Babette Deutsch (Age 10).

"Vincent Millay. E. Vincent Millay. By E. Vincent Millay," she whispered over and over to herself.

"Next time I'll sign my poems 'By E. Vincent Millay,'" she resolved.

She arrived in the schoolyard before the first bell had rung. Usually she came either at the last moment or late. A group of girls from the senior class were gathered in a tight, exclusive knot. She stood in awe of this august class. They seemed so old and knowing. Any impression she made on them would have to be done indirectly.

Vincent spied an unattached girl from the sophomore class, and hurried over immediately.

"Hi, there, Mary," she called in a cheerful voice. "Did you get your Latin done?"

"No, I didn't," Mary replied. "Could I look at your homework before we go in to class?"

Vincent stood irresolutely first on one foot and then on the other. Now was not the proper time to introduce her triumph, her masterpiece, her poem. Maybe there would be a better opportunity later in the study hall or between classes.

"There goes the first bell," Mary exclaimed. "Let's go." She bustled into the schoolhouse. Vincent followed rather reluctantly in her tow.

Vincent sat restlessly through the first two morning classes. She was so distracted she did not harass the teachers with her usual questions and arguments. She was waiting for her chance.

It came during the morning recess. A group of girls were gathered around Stella's desk. Vincent strolled over with a deceptively nonchalant air. She held the *St. Nicholas* magazine carefully under one arm.

There was a steady buzz of conversation. Vincent was too excited to pay any heed to it.

"Girls, girls!" she cried in a low, dramatic voice. "I have had a poem printed."

With this announcement, Vincent flung open the *St. Nicholas* magazine to the page where her poem appeared. The girls glanced momentarily at the magazine. It did not interest them much. They immediately returned to the discussion in which they were absorbed.

"What color did you say your new dress was going to be?" one girl asked Stella as if that were the most important thing in the world.

Stella answered complacently that it would be blue. The buzz of conversation resumed. Nobody paid any further attention to Vincent. Stella—generally so friendly and comforting and solid—was too absorbed in the description of her new dress to record Vincent's first triumph.

Nobody even glanced at Vincent's poem. With a hurt, crestfallen look of noncomprehension she turned away. Her narrow shoulders drooped pitifully.

"May I read your poem?"

It was Corinne, the new girl with red hair who had just come to Camden from a down-east village.

Wordlessly Vincent handed the magazine to Corinne.

"It's good. It's a very good poem," Corinne said slowly, reading it through twice.

Vincent knew she meant it. She had noticed in passing how pretty Corinne's dark auburn hair was and wished hers was the same shade. She also saw with awe and envy how dark and clearly defined Corinne's eyebrows were, while she had none, or rather hers were so light and thin they were invisible. Vincent felt a quick liking for Corinne and the two became fast friends.

Now Vincent was determined to achieve literary recognition, and she worked harder than ever on the school magazine. Month after month she continued to send in her contributions to the St. Nicholas League and steadily worked her way upward. As the year slowly passed, Mother Millay stood by with an ever-ready word of comfort and encouragement.

One day at school Vincent received a coveted promotion on the school newspaper and eager to share every little triumph with her mother, she hurried home to tell her the good news.

"Mother, I've just been appointed assistant editor in chief of *The Megunticook*," she announced, bursting into the sitting room where her mother was working on a transformation.

"How nice! How grand! I'm so glad for you, Sefe," Mrs. Millay said. "I knew you could do it."

"And then next year when I'm a senior, I'm almost sure to be editor in chief," Vincent added. "Unless, of course, I'm a simply terrible editor and they can't promote me."

"I'm sure you'll make a very good editor if you put your mind to it," Mrs. Millay said to calm Vincent's misgivings. "You've had a story or essay or poem in almost every issue since you were in the first term of your freshman year. And now you have a chance to show everybody what you can do."

"Yes," echoed Vincent darkly. "Now I'll have a chance to show them."

She still remembered the first time her name had appeared in the school magazine. *The Megunticook*, though published only three times during the school year, was impressively printed. The December, 1905, issue with its photographs of Camden scenery and landmarks was formidably grown up.

Vincent was the newest freshman then. She and Vivian Dodge had been selected to be the "local editors" for the freshman class. They were supposed to submit interesting items about the class of 1909. They worked conscientiously, keeping their ears and eyes open for the funny sayings or unintentional *faux pas* made in their classes.

Vincent and Vivian could scarcely wait for the first issue of the school magazine to appear in December. They were among the first eager buyers when it went on sale, holding their ten cents in readiness. Word by word, they read their own contributions under the local items. It was Vivian who discovered "The Newest Freshman" in print.

"Vincent, didn't you hand in an English composition called 'The Newest Freshman?'" Vivian asked. "Look on page 6. I think they've printed your essay."

Yes, there it was beginning in the second column of page 6. It spread over all of page 7 and a few words ran onto page 9. On the eighth page was a beautiful photograph of "The Mountain from Megunticook Lake." How wonderful to have her first printed essay surrounding such beauty.

Vincent sat down on a step in the school corridor to read her essay right then and there! Everything always looked so perfect when it was in print. She was almost at the bottom of the seventh page when a frown crossed her forehead. The word "eying" was incorrect. She knew she had spelled it properly in her paper. Here it was printed "eyeing." Everybody would make fun of her for that.

By the time she reached the end of the essay, she felt like crying. Her name was printed in block letters, but they had spelled it wrong.

Vivian was bubbling over with excitement. "You're the only freshman with an English composition in *The Megunticook*," she said. "Aren't you proud? Doesn't it make you happy?"

"No," Vincent answered shortly. "Look, they've printed my name wrong. Mill*ey*. I keep on telling the teachers it's spelled with an *a*."

Crestfallen, Vincent rose to go. She was not interested in the rest of the magazine. It was all spoiled for her now.

Vivian followed her with consoling words.

"Why don't you tell the editor in chief how to spell your name?" Vivian suggested. "Then any time they print it, you'll be sure it's right."

"Oh, I wouldn't dare," gasped Vincent.

Frank Evans was a senior and all of eighteen. Vincent—as a mere freshman—was afraid to approach so lofty a personage.

"Sure you can," Vivian encouraged her. "Sometime when you see him in the hall, just go up to him and tell him your name is spelled with an *a*. It's simple enough."

Vincent trembled. Frank Evans, in addition to being editor in chief of *The Megunticook*, was captain of the baseball team. He had written an account of the canoe trip through the Maine woods where he had gone with his brother the previous summer. Everyone expected that he would be valedictorian of the graduating class this year. How could she, Vincent Millay, stop this august and romantic older man of eighteen in the hall and tell him her name was spelled with an *a*.

"You could write him a note," Vivian suggested.

"No, that would be silly," reflected Vincent. "I'll go up to him sometime when we bring out local items and tell him myself—casually. What do you suppose I ought to call him? Mr. Evans? I'd never dare call him Frank."

"You don't have to call him anything," Vivian pointed out. "All you have to do is tell him."

Vincent was very grave and serious when she went in search of Frank Evans to hand him the freshman local items. She found him at last. He smiled absently from the lofty heights of eighteen at the shy little red-haired girl who gave him a sheaf of papers.

"My name was spelled wrong in *The Megunticook* last time," Vincent gulped. "My composition was printed and my last name is spelled with an *a*."

"And what is your name?" he inquired.

"Vincent Millay with an *a*," she answered.

Frank Evans made a quick note of it before he turned away to attend to the manifold duties and pleasures which clamored for his attention.

As March and the next issue of *The Megunticook* approached, Vincent and Vivian were in a turmoil of excitement. They wondered how many of the witticisms which they had submitted at the expense of other members of their class would be printed. Vincent was eager to see her name spelled correctly, too.

The Megunticook for March, 1906, surpassed all previous issues. The soft paper cover, thick and crinkled like leather, had a perfect circle cut in the middle of its elegant ecru expanse; through it could be seen the beautiful view of Sherman's Point which was reproduced on the title page. Vivian leafed through the advertisements quickly until they came to the page where the masthead was.

"What a lovely photograph of Negro Island," she exclaimed.

Vincent was busy reading the board of editors column. There it was. Editor in chief, Frank Evans. Assistant Editor in chief, Bertha Payson. Now the local editors. Two juniors. Two sophomores. Now Vivian's name and her name last.

"Oh, they've spelled my name worse than before—with two *a*'s and one *l*. Malay. It sounds like a disease," Vincent wailed. "What am I going to do?"

"You can't do anything about it now," Vivian pointed out.

"But I will do something," Vincent promised herself.

The next time she saw Frank Evans, Vincent resolutely confronted him in the school corridor.

"Mr. Evans—Frank Evans," she began in a tremulous voice, "I'm Vincent Millay, one of the local editors of the class of 1909. My name was spelled wrong again in *The Megunticook*. I've written it out so it will be right next time."

Breathless at the end of her long speech, Vincent handed him her card. Frank Evans absently took it from her trembling hand.

"Er-er, little girl, why don't you give this to Bertha Payson. She's assistant editor in chief and will take over the work in June. I'm going to be busy with baseball all this spring and then there'll be graduation. You'd better see Bertha, little girl."

With that, he handed back the slip of cardboard and made good his escape.

Vincent did see Bertha Payson. *The Megunticook* for June, 1906, had no beautiful scenic photograph on the masthead page, but her name was spelled correctly.

She smiled as she recalled her freshman troubles. They seemed long ago, when she was so very young.

Now Vincent, a junior, in her new position as assistant editor in chief, was preparing the December, 1907, issue of

The Megunticook for the press. Her duty was to read proof and no error escaped her eagle eye. If all went well, she was almost sure to take over the editorship from Leslie Arey in June.

She hurried home from the printer's with the galley proofs. It was bitterly cold in the little house in the hollow; Vincent was sniffling and sneezing. She resolved to get into bed and under the covers. There she could drink hot tea with lemon and correct the proofs as long as her rheumy eyes could see.

The names were all correct on the editorial board. She sighed. The boys on the magazine were such troublemakers. Perhaps when she was editor in chief, she would not have to keep George Frohock as athletic editor.

Vincent carefully read the essays, checking the occasional errors. "The One Session Question." "Tobacco and Its Users." "Value of Physical Culture in Our School." "How Sunday Should be Observed." "The Importance of Crossing T's." As quickly as she could she finished with all these earnest subjects.

She turned now to the Locals. They were still a favorite section of the magazine for her. That was how she had started as a freshman and occasionally she still contributed items.

She gripped her pencil and heavily marked a mistake. It was now punctuated exactly as she wanted it to be. She read the column with a faint smile.

"A new brilliant (?) poet has arisen in the junior class and his name is Mr. Frohock. This is his production; a poem sent to Miss Millay.

> 'Your nose is red
> And so is your head.'

"But he met his Waterloo in the following:

'There is a man in our town,
  And Oh! he is so wise,
To far Bombay and fair Cathay
  His wondrous knowledge flies.
He's much esteemed in Camden town.
  Of football he is king;
But his opinion of himself
  Surpasses everything.

'There's not a teacher in the school
  Who's half so smart as he,
With close-shut eyes his self-conceit
  We all can plainly see.
Be careful when you speak to him;
  Down on your knees and say,
"Please Mr. Frohock, may I have
  The right to live today?" '

Yes, this section of the Locals column was exactly as she wanted it. Vincent read further, checking every word carefully. Everything went smoothly for a while—no mistakes. Then she stopped again to rearrange a few lines. As she marked them, she whispered half aloud:

"Hark! What is that fearful sound,
  From the schoolhouse loudly ringing?
Are there guinea hens around?
  No that's Walter Conley singing
Like a Jew's-harp out of tune,
  Like a rusty fog horn blowing,
Wheezing like a croupy crow,
  Those melodious sounds are flowing."

She finished her proofreading in a few minutes. Soon she was asleep, breathing heavily.

NINE

Though Vincent worked hard on the school magazine, she did not neglect her piano lessons, for her ambitious goal was still the concert stage.

Mr. Tufts, her music teacher, was growing old. He was already half blind and she was his last pupil.

"How old are you now, Vincent?" Mr. Tufts asked as they finished an arduous lesson.

"Sixteen, my next birthday," she replied.

He took Vincent's hands, first the right and then the left, then pushed back thumb and little finger to their longest stretching point.

"Now see if you can do this," he instructed her, indicating the span he wanted her to reach on the piano.

Vincent nearly tore her fingers out of their sockets on the keyboard, but she could not span the octave.

Mr. Tufts shook his head sadly.

"Too bad, too bad," he muttered to himself.

She was puzzled, but not too concerned; Mr. Tufts had done this many times in the past year. Vincent's hands were tiny and doll like. As she put her sheet music into her case and turned to leave, she wished her hands were larger for Mr. Tufts's sake almost more than her own.

"Tell your mother to come with you next time, Vincent," Mr. Tufts called after her. "I want to talk to her."

Mrs. Millay accompanied her daughter to the next lesson. Together they sat stiffly on the sofa until Mr. Tufts suggested that Vincent play her Mozart piece.

When she had finished, he groped his way to the piano. Facing Mrs. Millay with tears streaming down his face he said, "In all the years I've been teaching and composing, I hoped to develop one really fine musician to give to the world. It would have given my own life a reason for existence."

He took both of Vincent's hands and held them against his face. His tears were coursing down freely now.

"It is not to be. It is not to be," the music teacher continued. "Vincent is my last pupil and her hands are too small. She will never be a great pianist."

"Are you sure? Isn't there anything to be done?" Mrs. Millay asked. She was on the verge of tears herself.

"Perhaps a surgical operation might help. It is hard to tell."

Mrs. Millay gasped. Vincent shuddered.

When they reached home, both of them wept.

"Perhaps Mr. Tufts is wrong," Mrs. Millay consoled her, after the worst of the storm had subsided. "Maybe you ought to play for someone else."

"No, he is right," Vincent answered stonily. "I'll never be a great pianist."

Her mother put in softly. "Nothing is wasted. You can always play for your own pleasure as I do. Or maybe someday you'll write a great poem about music. Poetry is as important as music. A poem can be about anything you've experienced—music, geometry, a tree, a mountain, a boat. No experience is ever wasted."

"Poets never become rich, Mother. They always starve," observed Vincent quite sensibly. "I'll write poetry because I love it—because something in me must—but a poet doesn't make money."

"Then be an actress. Everyone in high school likes your acting," Mrs. Millay suggested.

Vincent seemed to be satisfied with this; she would become famous as a poetess or rich *and* famous as an actress.

"Vincent, are you listening to me?" she heard her mother's voice from afar as in a dream. "I want you to continue your piano lessons. You can pay for the lessons with the money you made working in Mr. Montgomery's law office."

The summer before, when Vincent was fifteen years old, she had worked as a typist in Job Montgomery's office. At fifteen it made her feel very important to set out for the village each morning, armed with a sheaf of papers and sharpened pencils, ready to display her newly acquired skills in stenography and typewriting, a course she had taken that year in high school. Vincent felt herself a part of the great working world, a cog in the machine, and very grown up to be earning money.

Mr. Montgomery was an amateur poet as well as a lawyer, and sometimes he and Vincent compared their efforts. Eager to try new and intricate verse forms, Vincent wrote her first sonnet that summer. It was a poem about old letters, yellowed with age, that she was intent on burning. Mr. Montgomery pointed out doubtfully that the subject was not too suitable for a girl of her age—for what letters, yellow with age, would she have to burn and try to forget at fifteen—but he read eagerly some of the lines which contained real feeling. Vincent was fascinated by the difficult rhyme pattern of the sonnet and resolved to perfect herself in it.

Her employer often talked about having a book of his poems published at his own expense. Vincent said nothing, only lifting her neatly coifed head quizzically. Even though she was only fifteen and he was a grown man, she knew she would never publish her poems out of her own earnings. A professional poet must be accepted by a real publisher, she knew, and when a book of her poems was published, that is the way it would have to be. She might never become rich as a poetess, but perhaps she could be famous. She would use her earnings for piano lessons as her mother suggested, and there might be riches in store for her as an actress.

Vincent's thoughts were a thousand miles away. She pictured herself as a famous actress. Her gowns would be resplendent. There would be dozens of them—in all the colors of the rainbow and with suitable wigs. Always, she was the heroine—sweet, winning and charming. The footlights would blaze as she spoke her lines; then would come the endless applause. After the play, her dressing room would be filled with banks of flowers from myriad admirers.

At her mother's insistence Vincent did continue piano lessons with Mrs. Leila Bucklin French, but they were never the same after that day. She could become a good pianist but she knew she would never be great.

Vincent soon had the chance to prove herself as an actress on a real stage. During her junior year in school the class decided to present a play instead of the usual Junior Exhibition. Clutching the script, Vincent waited for her turn to read. She wanted the title role of Gypsy, the mountain waif. She glanced at Stella, who also wanted to be the heroine. Stella had already read the part of Gypsy aloud—very well, too, Vincent had to admit.

Now it was her turn. Vincent walked to the front of the room and opened the book at the scene she was to read. She declaimed her lines with passion; every gesture had been carefully rehearsed. She finished and took her seat again.

"Anyone else for Gypsy?" Mr. Wells asked without raising his eyes from the paper on which he wrote down the names of the aspirants.

There were no other candidates for the role. Mr. Wells held a hurried consultation with the teachers who were serving as judges.

"Stella Derry will be Gypsy, the mountain waif," he announced.

Vincent could not believe her ears—Stella, not she, had the leading role.

"Why don't you try for the role of the Irishwoman, Vincent?" suggested Mr. Wells. "It's a character role that calls for real acting ability."

Vincent could scarcely fight back her disappointment. She agreed to read through the part, though it was not at all to her taste. It was primarily a comedy role. She would be "Mike's irritable wife" and have a grandchild.

Vincent went to the front of the room again and read the part lackadaisically. As she read on she found herself becoming interested in it. She could practice a real Irish brogue. She might be able to enliven the scenes by beating Mike—whoever he was to be—over the head with a broom. Yes, the part did have its possibilities. As soubrette she would have been merely sweet and charming. In this character role she could really act.

No one else tried for the role of the terrible-tempered Irishwoman and the part was automatically awarded to her. Now all the female parts were taken except for the small grandchild.

"Does anyone know a little girl about ten or eleven years old who could take the part of the grandchild?" Mr. Wells asked.

Vincent's hand shot up instantly.

"My sister Kathleen can. She's a very good little actress," she informed him eagerly.

"Bring her to the first rehearsal and we'll see how she does," replied Mr. Wells. "Now all the girls are dismissed."

At the first rehearsal, Kathleen was tested for the role of the grandchild. She was already letter perfect in the lines; Vincent had seen to that. She won the part easily.

The girls were all ranged on one side of the room, the boys on the other. Mr. Wells read off the complete cast of characters and the actors. The girls all nudged Stella when they learned who the hero would be. How relieved Vincent was now that she did not have the soubrette role. Imagine having to kiss George Frohock and pretend to be in love with him.

The rehearsal began. The play seemed hopeless; every member appeared to be miscast.

"We have a lot of work to do to get this play in shape before December 6," Mr. Wells told them seriously. "Everybody must work hard in the few weeks we have and attend every rehearsal."

The Camden Opera House was ablaze with lights on the night of December 6. Almost four hundred people were crowded inside the auditorium. Vincent held Kathleen's hand as she peered out from behind the curtain. There was Mother Millay in the center of the third row with Norma beside her.

Vincent was already wearing her heavy make-up and ludicrous clothes. For the occasion, she had also surreptitiously blackened her eyebrows (which were normally an invisible blond) with soot from the bottom of the kettle.

When Vincent walked onto the stage, there was a momentous pause. She began to speak her lines and act her part. She felt an electric thrill of contact with the audience. She knew they were hers, following intently every word she spoke and every move she made.

I'm good, she thought with an impersonal awareness of herself. I can do anything I want to with the audience out there.

And there was applause—endless applause. It was a sweeter triumph than Vincent had dreamed.

The play was such a success that the Pythian sisters presented it again at the Opera House on May 8, with Mr. Wells in the role of Mike. In reviewing the play, the local paper said he was at his best in Irish comedy. "His stage partner Vincent Millay was excellent," the notice read. "Their amusing love scenes caught the audience."

During her senior year the class play was *The Brookdale Mystery*, which was given on a drizzly evening the night before Thanksgiving. This time Vincent had the soubrette role. George Frohock was the villain. Stella was the second soubrette.

The class earned only forty dollars, though everyone said it was a better play than *Gypsy*. That gave Vincent pause for thought. She had been thinking about New York and becoming rich as a famous actress. Perhaps the theater was not the easiest way to fame and fortune after all.

TEN

It scarcely seemed possible to Vincent that she was now an august senior. Her freshman days seemed so long ago. Nobody had known her then, for she had come into high school on trial. Now she was editor in chief of *The Megunticook,* an important personage in high school affairs.

Strange. She had not done the many retaliatory things she had planned. George Frohock was still athletic editor. She hadn't been able to dismiss him; her sense of fair play would not let her. She had even appointed Walter Conley local editor for the junior class in place of someone who had left school. None of the other editors would have been generous enough to print a poem by Henry Hall. Vincent wrinkled her nose as she read it. It began:

A Summer Idyl

A maid with brown and laughing eyes,
The cause of many regretful sighs . . .

She did not want anybody to accuse her of putting only her own poetry into the magazine, and wondered if they would know who had written the poem signed E. V. M. She glanced through it hastily, saying the words to herself and wishing she had more time to work on the first and last stanzas:

As Others See Us

Oh, the Freshman miss has timid feet,
She tiptoes in from the door to her seat,
But Pickled limes by the dozen she'll eat
    With her eyes on the teacher's glasses:

Oh, the Senior miss has a memory short,
Her Freshman days she has quite forgot,
She may have been one she remembers it not,
    Her dignity's very surprising.

The Megunticook was going to press soon. She marked the last period carefully and hoped everybody would like it.

Now it was time for the class meeting, which was becoming increasingly serious. As seniors, it was not too soon for them to start planning their graduation. Spring drew near and there was a class meeting almost every week. The one Vincent was going to now was important—they were going to choose the honor parts for graduation.

The president of the class rapped for order. The seniors settled down more or less quietly in their seats. It was explained that the class parts would be selected from among the honor students.

"What shall we do about the valedictorian and salutatorian?" he asked the class. "One of the teachers didn't keep numerical grades for the class and there is no way of telling the exact ranks."

Vincent's hand shot up. The president of the class recognized her and she rose to speak. The boys in the class began shouting and stamping their feet. She could not make herself heard above the din, so she sat down.

Howard Beedy, a new boy who had only been in the senior class a short time, now had the floor. A tall, blond boy, who was a splendid athlete and good student, Howard was well liked by everybody.

"I've noticed that whenever a certain person gets up to speak in class meeting, there's such a noise that nobody can hear what she wants to say," he began somewhat angrily. "Now it seems to me that it isn't very fair. Sometimes that person might have a good suggestion. How can we tell, if we don't get a chance to listen?"

Howard sat down abruptly. There was a shamed silence in the room.

Vincent then proposed that since no one knew exactly who should be valedictorian and salutatorian because of the missing grades, those two parts should be omitted from graduation. The proposal was unanimously accepted.

Now they moved on to the business of electing a class historian, orator, someone to do the class prophecy, and the class poet. They decided to choose them from among the entire class—those who had honor parts and those who did not—on the basis of merit and ability.

"Nominations for class historian are now in order," the president of the class announced.

"I nominate William Hanley," one of the boys said.

"I second the motion," said another.

"I move the nominations be closed," said the first boy when no additional names were put forward.

"Second the motion," chorused everybody.

William Hanley is unanimously elected class historian," the president announced.

One of the girls nominated Mary Pendleton to give the class prophecy. She was unanimously elected.

Harold Nash was unanimously elected class orator.

"Nominations are in order for class poet," the president called automatically.

"I nominate Vincent Millay," said Corinne.

"I second the motion," Stella called out above the voices of the other girls.

"I move . . ."

"Wait a minute!" It was the loud voice of George making himself heard above the shrill soprano voices of the girls. "I nominate Henry Hall for class poet."

"I second the nomination," came the chorus of heavy male voices.

Vincent looked around quickly. It was a plot, she knew. There were thirteen boys in the class and only eight girls. At least twelve of the boys would vote for Henry Hall.

It really was not fair, she thought passionately to herself. They had said those parts would be awarded on merit and ability. She had had stories and poems in almost every issue of *The Megunticook* since she was a first-term freshman. The only poem of Henry Hall's that had been printed was the one that she herself had accepted when she was editor in chief. Everyone in the class knew that she had had six poems published in the *St. Nicholas* magazine. When she had won a gold badge for "The Land of Romance," her mother had taken the poem to the Camden *Herald* and it had been reprinted in the newspaper. Afterward *The Megunticook* had printed it, too, with this notation:

The following poem, written by one of our High School Students, won first prize in the *St. Nicholas* magazine contest and was published in the March number of that magazine:

"Show me the road to Romance!" I cried, and he raised
   his head;
"I know not the road to Romance, child. 'Tis a warm
   bright way," he said.
"And I trod it once with one whom I loved—with one
   who is long since dead.

"But now—I forget,—Ah! The way would be long with-
    out that other one."
And he lifted a long and trembling hand, to shield his
    eyes from the sun.

"Show me the road to Romance!" I cried, but she did
    not stir,
And I heard no sound in the low-ceilinged room save
    the spinning wheels busy whirr.

Then came a voice from the down-bent head, from lips
    that I could not see,
"Oh, why do you seek for Romance? And why do you
    trouble me?
"Little care I for your fancies. They will bring you no
    good," she said.
"Take the wheel that stands in the corner, and get you
    to work instead."

Then came one with steps so light that I had not heard
    their tread,
"I know where the road to Romance is, I will show it to
    you," she said.
She slipped her tiny hand in mine, and smiled up into
    my face,
And lo! A ray of the setting sun shone full upon the
    place.
The little brook danced down the hill and the grass
    sprang up anew.
And tiny flowers peeped forth as fresh as if newly
    washed with snow.

A little breeze came frolicking by, cooling the heated air,
And the road to Romance stretched on before, beckon-
    ing bright and fair.

And I knew that just beyond it, in the hush of the dying
    day,
The mossy walls and ivied towers of the land of Ro-
    mance lay.
The breath of dying lilies haunted the twilight air,
And the sob of a dreaming violin filled the silence every-
    where.

After this, everyone in school had known that she had
gained some recognition as a poet. The awful thing was that
Henry Hall really did not care about being the class poet.
Vincent knew the boys were doing it to be mean. She would
have to think of some way to show them up.

"I withdraw my name from the nomination," Vincent said
in her sweetest voice while these thoughts were racing
through her head.

"Oh, Vincent! What do you want to do that for?" a few
girls protested.

"Let's vote. Let's vote," urged some of the boys.

"No, I withdraw my name from the nomination," Vincent
repeated firmly. "I think the election of class poet should be
unanimous like the others."

Everyone looked at Henry Hall. He sat there doing and
saying nothing. There was a sheepish expression on his face.

The president of the class stood first on one foot and then
on the other.

"No, we want to vote," came a voice from the male section
of the room.

"I withdraw my name from the nomination," Vincent
repeated again.

Henry Hall was unanimously elected class poet.

Vincent went home holding her head high. But she was
heartbroken. She was an honor student and nobody could
vote that away from her. As an honor student, she was sup-

posed to write and recite an essay for the graduation ceremonies.

On graduation night, the class of 1909 sat stiffly in their
chairs in a semicircle on the stage of the Camden Opera
House—the eight girls in front and the thirteen boys in back.
Vincent looked out into the sea of faces to catch a glimpse
of her mother, with Kathleen on one side and Norma on the
other. Vincent closed her eyes and said the opening lines of
her essay to herself. She had committed it to memory very
carefully and rehearsed every gesture. Some people were
going to be very surprised when they heard it.

When the Reverend Sylvanus Frohock finished the
prayer, Martha Knight gave her essay on "Scottish Folk
Minstrels." The class history was recounted by William
Joseph Hanley. Stella Lee Derry played a piano solo, "The
Messengers of Spring." Now it was time for Vincent's essay.
The program said, Poem, *La Joie de Vivre*—Edna St. Vincent
Millay.

When she rose to recite, her appearance did not matter.
The tiny red-haired girl in the homemade white graduation
dress seemed to transcend herself and grow larger as she
declaimed in thrilling tones:

" ' Tis good to be alive a day like this!
' Tis good to be alive! I will not miss
One joy from out the living; I will go
Through valleys low, where deepset mountains throw
A shadow and a shelter from the heat,
In cool retreat where shall no city street
Intrude its noise and scare the stillness sweet.

Deep draw I in my breath,
   Deep drink of water cold;
   There is no growing old,
There is no death.

The world and I are young!
   Never on the lips of man
   Never since time began
Has gladder song been sung."

It was a long poem, but the audience sat absorbed until she had recited it to the end and returned to her place among the other graduates. There was almost an awed moment of silence before the audience applauded. Vincent knew she had done well, for she had put all of herself into it.

Now the entire school sang "The Lord is Great." Vincent was carried along on the surge of music. She needed it; otherwise she might have burst out crying.

Mary Pendleton—motherly, dependable Mary Pendleton—gave the class prophecy next. Toward the end, Vincent heard her voice come through clearly as she said, "Vincent. Last but not least are you, Vincent, and do you recall the old saying that the best is reserved for the last. There is much for you to accomplish in the future, so much for your cease-less ambition to urge you to. Your writing, dramatic ability and also your singing will serve to assist you in gaining a high position in the world."

Then came more music by the orchestra and Henry Hall read the class poem, "Our Destiny." It was pale and imitative compared to Vincent's poem and to her delivery. Through a haze, Vincent heard the next essay and then Guy Blood's cornet solo. Howard Beedy read his essay and the class ode was sung to the tune of "Santa Lucia."

Harold Newton presented the gifts. Vincent received a book on argumentation because she argued so much. She was stung but could do nothing.

The next moment, she had her triumph. Mr. Packard, the superintendent, called her name and asked her to step for-ward. Vincent came to the center of the stage once more.

"It gives me great pleasure to announce," Mr. Packard began, "that Miss Millay's original poem has been awarded the prize for the best essay by a member of the graduating class."

He handed her a bright and shining ten-dollar gold piece. Nothing that Vincent had ever received before meant as much to her. In spite of all her troubles and humiliations, she was graduating from high school in a blaze of glory.

She returned to her seat. Mr. Packard now called the name of each graduate and as they came forward, one by one, he awarded the diplomas to the class.

Graduation ended with a benediction. It was over. Vincent was so glad and so tired.

ELEVEN

At seventeen, Vincent considered herself grown up. Her long hair was done up in a bun and she was a graduate of Camden High School. She would have liked to have gone away to college, but she knew it was an impossible dream. Too frail to work steadily, she was an occasional salesgirl at the Village Gift Shop during the busy seasons; a part-time stenographer for summer people; a junior secretary in the law office of Mr. Job Montgomery, her erstwhile employer of two years back, who also wrote poetry.

It was much easier for Mother Millay now that the girls were growing up and Vincent was earning some money. They moved to a better house directly across from the high school. Vincent was thrilled. It had paint on its clapboards like any other house—beautiful white paint and neat green shutters. The first day they lived there she kept running outside to touch the paint on the clapboards. She thought back to her housekeeping in the little weather-beaten house in the hollow. They had been so carefree and happy there, she missed it a little already. It was part of her childhood and she was growing up.

Vincent still dreamed of fame, but now that she was older she realized it would not come at seventeen or eighteen or nineteen. She worked at her poetry and she still wanted to try to be an actress. There were amateur theatricals in Camden and she nearly always had roles. She played the lead in *Pygmalion and Galatea* and had her picture taken in her costume—a beautiful Grecian gown. Her hair was piled high on her head and encircled with gleaming metallic bands. At the Camden Opera House, there were sometimes traveling stock companies that presented plays professionally. Vincent obtained a part in one and even went to another town with the company. She hoped for more, but in the end there were no further roles for her.

She still sent her poems to the St. Nicholas League. She was entitled to do so only for a few months more until she would be eighteen. The month she was eighteen years old, the magazine printed this poem in its Letters-to-the-Editor section:

Hope

by Edna von der Heide (Age 18. Alas!)

The gray dawn breaks within the eastern sky;
  The pallid moon wanes slowly in the west;
  The morning steals upon a world at rest;
And I, must say "Good-by."

The pearly dew still to the grasses clings,
  Where brilliant beams of rose and amethyst
  Unroll through cold, damp thicknesses of mist
The hope of brighter things.

Now that Vincent was too old to send her poems to the St. Nicholas League, it was like a door to the outside world suddenly slammed shut in her face. She had already looked farther afield for success, but the grown-up world was difficult and discouraging. Three years ago the April issue of the magazine *Current Literature* had printed and reviewed her poem, "The Land of Romance," with the following comment by Edward Wheeler:

"The poem which follows (by E. St. Vincent Millay)

seems to me to be phenomenal. The author, whether boy or girl we do not know, is just fourteen years of age."

Since then she had flooded the mails with her poems to literary magazines, but none had been accepted. How long could she continue to beat her head against a stone wall? she wondered. Camden was breath-taking in its beauty. Yet a young girl could not live merely on beautiful scenery, for life, after all, was not a play. Camden was a quiet backwater and Vincent longed for the life of the outside world. She felt stifled in the narrow little town; sometimes it seemed as though she were buried alive. Yet her hope renewed itself eternally. A wonderful day would lift her spirits, an exciting thunderstorm would clear the air, or a glimpse of hidden beauty in the flight of a bird or the perfection of a tiny pebble would come her way. Then life would seem worth living again and it was good to be young and alive.

Kathleen and Norma were both in high school now. Norma was extremely pretty—the prettiest of the three sisters with her red-gold, fluffy hair and milky skin. The house was always full of girls and boys. Now that Vincent was older, she, too, enjoyed the company of some of the young men from Camden and the neighboring towns. There were fudge parties and impromptu suppers at their house which was a gathering place for the high school students across the way. Vincent sometimes played the piano and they sang far into the night.

In the winter there was skating on the lakes and ponds and sleigh rides through the hills wooded with evergreen trees. At the first signs of spring, Vincent and her friends went to the swamplands for pussy willows. On week ends they organized expeditions to Mount Battie to search for the first mayflowers of the season. In the summer there was swimming. One wonderful summer when Vincent was nine-teen, there were several moonlight picnics at which they built bonfires on the beach and baked clams or roasted corn. Once they took her treasured chafing dish to Sherman's Point in a motor boat called *The Frolic,* packing it carefully in a hatbox. At Sherman's Point they concocted a delicious shrimp wiggle. There were five girls on the picnic that night—Ethel, Martha, Norma, Vincent and Emma. The phosphorous on the water was brilliant; there were spots of it as large as silver dollars. When the picnic was over, Jake called for them in *The Frolic,* towing Norma and Emma in the tender in which they had rowed over to the Point.

Another day, Mr. Knight, the father of one of Vincent's friends, hired *The India,* a large motorboat belonging to Mr. Elwell for an all-day picnic. There were fourteen—not counting Mr. and Mrs. Elwell. They started at eight o'clock in the morning and did not get home until eleven o'clock at night. They sailed in and around the islands in Camden Bay to Pulpit Harbor where they landed on a small uninhabited island. Vincent felt like Robinson Crusoe. There were about twenty things to eat: fish chowder on the boat before they landed; baked clams and boiled lobsters on shore; all kinds of sandwiches and cake; plums, peaches and pears; and on the way home an enormous watermelon, salted almonds, chocolates, wafers and gum. They caught the codfish for the chowder in the deep water of the bay before they sailed into Pulpit Harbor. Gladys caught a haddock and Jake a large pollack. There were two hooks on each line and they had to be unwound for what seemed miles before they reached the end. Then the lines struck bottom and had to be pulled up again about three feet. Martha and Vincent each caught two good-sized cod. Then Martha caught two at once so Vincent, of course, was eager to equal the exploit. After much patient waiting, she hauled in her double catch— only to find that one was a dogfish and the other a sculpin. They all roared with laughter at her catch and she, too, joined in the general derision. Mr. Knight unhooked them both for her—with much care, since dogfish are poisonous and sculpins very ugly to look at—and threw them back into the ocean. Jake and Martha (who had both brought cameras) snapped pictures all day long. The seven girls all wore middy blouses and farmer hats and posed for one picture lying flat on their stomachs, with their elbows on the ground, chin in hands and feet in the air. They decided to call the picture "We Are Seven." It was a happy crowd that returned across the moonlit bay that night.

In her worst moments of discouragement, Vincent always remembered that happy summer and its good times, for she had been discouraged since her graduation from high school. Her life seemed to be going nowhere and she was restless in Camden.

At eighteen she felt closed in by the mountains that rimmed the seaside town, and often tried to escape her strange moods by climbing to the top of her favorite mountain. There she could breathe and feel free.

It was not yet four o'clock one morning when she crept from her bed to dress. The day was gray and still. She wanted to go to the summit of Mount Megunticook to watch the sun rise. When she reached the top, the first white fingers of dawn streaked against the leaden sky. Vincent looked down. She saw the long blue mountains and a forest through the mist. She turned toward the bay and saw the islands. They looked like black spots on the dark water. She reached up her hand toward the low-hanging, heavy clouds. It almost seemed as if she could touch the sky.

Her hand was so heavy, it seemed to weigh her down. The feeling of being buried alive overwhelmed her. Then there was a sudden squall. She smelled the apples of last autumn in the rain. The shower stopped as suddenly as it had begun;

the burning rays of the sun showed fiery red in the sky. Vincent felt new—as if she had just been reborn.

She began writing the words of a new poem. Words and verses were missing here and there. She paid no heed but wrote on until she had no more words. She wanted to express her feelings up there on the mountain. The words came tumbling out as she scribbled.

It was a long poem. Since Vincent knew she could not finish it then and there, she tucked the rumpled paper into her pocket. She was exalted. This poem might be *the* one about the mountain; her feeling for it was still very special. Now that she was eighteen, perhaps she could write a poem big enough for the mountain.

When she showed the poem to her mother at last, Mrs. Millay was enthusiastic.

"I think it's the best poem you've ever written, Sefe," her mother said emphatically.

"But I can't finish it," wailed Vincent. "I can't make it say exactly how I felt up there on the mountain."

"You will be able to finish it later on," Mrs. Millay said comfortingly. "Perhaps when you're a little older, you'll be better able to express your feelings."

"I don't think I'll ever be able to do it," replied Vincent with a woebegone expression on her face.

"Sure you will," her mother encouraged her. "It will come to you someday. Just put it away for a while."

Vincent put this poem away carefully in a drawer and every few months she took it up and read it again. There were some lines that were perfect. Here and there she changed words or rewrote entire lines. She decided she would never show it to anybody until it was as perfect as she could make it.

She wrote many little poems about the fields and the hills, the flowers and the sea around her. However, she had no place to send them with any assurance that they would be printed. She sorely missed the St. Nicholas League, where she had been awarded every possible prize. The grown-up magazines did not seem to want to print her poems.

"Just the same, I'll keep sending them out," she told herself. "One poem of mine was printed in *Current Literature* and I was paid for it. Perhaps there will be others."

Mr. Montgomery, her occasional employer since the summer she had worked in his law office when she was fifteen, still talked of having a book of his poems printed—at his own expense, of course. Vincent wondered idly what it would be like to have a whole book of poems printed "by E. Vincent Millay."

It was all right for Mr. Montgomery to talk—he was rich. Vincent again decided she wouldn't want it that way.

I'd like to have a publisher put out a book of my poems, she thought secretly. Then I'd be a *real* poet—not just someone who *thought* she was a poet.

As Vincent's nineteenth birthday came and went and fame still eluded her, she was more and more discouraged. While it was nice in Camden, she hoped she wouldn't have to stay there the rest of her life.

It was with a feeling of foreboding that Vincent extracted the letter from Kingman, Maine, from the mailbox. She wondered what news it would bring. Throughout most of her life, her father had remained a shadowy figure. She remembered well enough his sandy hair, the rosy complexion she had inherited from him, the bright blue eyes. Though there was a frequent correspondence and some visiting, it was almost like getting a letter from a long-lost relative. She really hadn't a very clear idea of what sort of man he really was or what other people thought of him. Her only consistent impression of him was the many times a twenty-dollar bill would fall from the envelope for something special the three sisters wanted—if he had been lucky at cards.

Vincent fingered the letter a few moments before opening it; she did not know why she was so reluctant. When she finally opened it and read its contents, a cry of pity escaped her.

Father was ill! Poor Father! All alone and in great pain with nobody to care for him. How desperately lonely he must be! She was the logical person to go to him, of course. She was not working for the time being; Mother Millay was. Norma and Kathleen could not miss high school. Yes, she decided, she would go to help nurse her father through his illness.

Mrs. Millay, too, was in favor of the plan. She and Henry were still on friendly terms. Sometimes she wondered if she hadn't misjudged him and been a little hasty.

Traveling to Kingman from Camden in the wintertime was a problem. Vincent took a roundabout and cumbersome route, finally finishing the last few miles by sleigh.

She was an excellent companion in the sickroom. What she lacked in technical knowledge, she made up in kindness and faithfulness. This suffering man, whose courage and spirit she so admired, was her father. His ideas were big and his ambition boundless—like her own. He was a dreamer. Perhaps if he had been more practical he could have been a great business success. He was not lacking in ability. People said that he could sell insurance—or anything else—to practically anybody. His difficulty was that he was too trusting. He lacked the toughness it required to collect the payments. Yet Vincent would not have had him otherwise. It was only when he was so near death that she realized how much she loved him and had missed having him as a father. He was kind—and even at the worst times of the crisis he would not trouble anyone more than was necessary. There was always a smile and a kind thank-you on his lips for her. The brush with death deepened Vincent's sensitivity.

When his illness passed, Vincent felt that she had truly left her childhood behind her. She had spent her twentieth birthday watching her father struggle for his life. If only her mother could see Father Millay as she had seen him and could hear how well the townspeople of Kingman thought of him, perhaps she would realize the measure of the man and forgive his faults more readily.

In another sickroom in faraway Camden, Mother Millay sat on the night watch. The patient was quiet; the room was tidy and clean. All the little tasks had been done. She looked around for something to read.

In the wastebasket she spied a discarded copy of *The Forum* magazine. It was worn and ragged, but she thumbed through it idly. Now she stopped at the half-torn page of an advertisement. It was a circular for a poetry contest sponsored by *The Lyric Year*—an annual book which would publish the one hundred best contemporary poems submitted each year. The first prize was five hundred dollars.

Mrs. Millay immediately tore the advertisement out of the magazine. She felt about in the half-light until she found paper and pen and ink. Enclosing the half-torn circular, she wrote Vincent a letter urging her to come home and finish her long poem about the mountain. The deadline was not far off.

Vincent came home to Camden as soon as she could; her father had long since recovered. She had been staying on, enjoying Kingman and its people.

"This is your big chance," her mother said when the greetings were over.

When she was alone, Vincent took out the long poem. It was not as unfinished as she had thought. She understood more about life, she mused, now that she had been so close to death. She worked faithfully and hard. At last, "Renascence" was finished—as perfect as she could ever make it. She sent it off to *The Lyric Year* contest with a hope and a prayer.

In a few months she received a letter from Mr. Ferdinand Pinney Earle, the editor and one of the judges of the contest. He wrote how much he liked "Renascence" and said he was going to vote it the first prize.

Vincent was overjoyed. Five hundred dollars would mean so much. She could go away to college for two years or more. It seemed too good to be true.

It was. When the votes were counted, her poem won only fourth place and an honorable mention. Mr. Earle had voted it first place but the other two judges had not voted for it at all. It would be printed in the annual volume of *The Lyric Year*.

To have been so near to winning—to have thought that she had won—the disappointment was terrible! She almost wished she hadn't tried at all.

"But it's still a great poem, Sefe," her mother told her. "Mr. Earle thought so—and others will, too. You'll see."

But Vincent could not be consoled.

TWELVE

"But I don't want to go to the party," Vincent wailed. "Why don't you ask a boy?"

"Oh, Vincent, don't be like that," Norma said urgently. "You'll feel better if you come to the party. I'll make you a darling costume. It will be fun, you'll see."

"I don't know why you have to have me there," Vincent assented rather grudgingly.

"We can waltz together," Norma assured her eagerly. "There's going to be a waltz prize and a prize for the best costume. . . ."

"All right. All right," Vincent agreed wearily. "I'll go, but you can't convince me I'll enjoy it."

Norma had waited on tables at the Whitehall Inn all summer. As the season neared its end, the summer people gave a big party for the help. Each waitress could invite one person and Norma insisted that Vincent come as her guest. She busily set about planning her costume and Vincent's, lavishing even more care and thought on what Vincent would wear than on her own.

The night of the party was one of those heady, winelike evenings that are frequent along the Maine coast in late August. Whitehall Inn was ablaze with lights. Japanese lanterns were strung out of doors over the ample side veranda. The band was already playing when Vincent and Norma arrived. Norma looked her pink-cheeked best as a simple country maiden. Vincent was resplendent in a lavender pierrette costume with her bright red hair flowing to her waist.

The two of them surveyed the gay scene for a few moments. The bright colors of the costumes and the festive lights were memorable. Then they joined in the dancing. At first they danced with each other, then they danced with some of the local young men who had come with the other girls or with the summer guests. For the first time since her great disappointment, Vincent began to feel alive. It was good to be young and gay and dancing.

"Everybody get ready for the waltz contest," announced Walter Geier, who was acting as master of ceremonies.

"Come on, Vincent. We have to waltz together," Norma said instantly. "I'll lead you."

The music began. The gaily costumed couples waltzed around the room and out under the stars on the wide, open veranda. Vincent and Norma waltzed as they never had before. They felt as if they were dancing on air. Other couples were tapped on the shoulder and gradually dropped out. Soon there were only a few dancers left. Vincent and Norma glided lightly and gracefully under the softly glowing lanterns. Now there was one other couple left, and when they, too, were eliminated, only Vincent and Norma were left dancing to the last strains of the waltz. The music stopped.

"Everybody in line for the grand march for the best costume," Walter Geier called out. "After the grand march there will be a short intermission with entertainment."

The summer visitors, the help and guests all lined up obligingly for the grand march. The band struck up a marching tune and the masqueraders walked around in single file. There were fishermen in yellow slickers, boots and sou'wester oiled hats. There were babies in frilled bonnets who stood close to six feet tall and had heavy muscular legs

and arms. Tramps hobnobbed with queens. Grotesque clowns
jostled fierce buccaneers. Vincent was an appealing figure
in her exquisite lavender pierrette costume. She was tiny
and her lightness and sprightliness gave her an elfin charm.
Now she was glad she had come; she hadn't a care in the
world.

With a fanfare and a long roll of the drums, the grand
march ended and the master of ceremonies announced the
prizes.

"Dance prize—Norma Millay," he called in a loud voice.

Norma came forward, bowed and accepted her prize with
the bouquet of flowers that went with it.

Then Walter announced the prizes for the funniest costume, the most fantastic costume and the most original
costume.

"Prettiest costume—Miss Vincent Millay," he called next.

Vincent was surprised, and Norma had to push her toward
the makeshift stand to receive her prize.

During the intermission there was entertainment, and
suddenly Vincent heard herself being called on to play and
sing.

She entered into the spirit of the evening. She came forward readily and sat down at the piano. Norma sat on the
floor behind the piano and coached Walter. He asked
Vincent if she would play and sing "Humoresque" and the
"Circus Rag," her own compositions.

Vincent sang a plaintive, sweet tune in her small, true
voice—a lovely song of summer butterflies and flowers. It
was well received with generous applause and Vincent
acknowledged it with a bow.

"Now Miss Millay will render "The Circus Rag," Walter
said with a grin.

Vincent sat down at the piano again and played the
prelude. She piped briskly for the steam calliope effect and

started singing the lively verses. It was a comic song and quite jazzy. It told the story of children at the circus—exhorted by a circus barker to step right up, one for a quarter. Soon everyone was tapping feet in time to the music and joining in the lively refrain describing the barker as

". . . that old windbag,
A-chewing the circus rag."

When Vincent rose to take her bow, the applause was resounding. The summer guests and the help crowded around her to beg for "one more." She had to repeat the song again and still they were not satisfied.

One summer visitor came up to her at the piano and asked, "Is that a new song? Where did you get it? I've never heard it before, and I thought I'd heard everything."

"I made it up," Vincent said, modestly lowering her eyes.

"Both the words and the music!" he exclaimed in surprise.

Vincent nodded wordlessly.

"Do you have anything else you can do now?" he asked.

"I have a new poem," she said. "It's going to be printed soon in *The Lyric Year*."

The guests were still applauding and calling for more entertainment from Vincent Millay.

She turned halfway around on the piano stool facing the audience, a tiny figure in her costume, with loose red hair swirling in gentle waves below her waist. As soon as there was absolute silence, she said simply, "Renascence."

She recited the poem from beginning to end. No one except her family had heard it before. Though it was an exceedingly long poem the guests were spellbound, and when she had finished there was a long hush, then tumultuous applause.

Vincent slipped away. She and Norma hurried toward the punch bowl for drinks and cookies and tried to lose themselves in the crowd but everybody kept coming up to congratulate Vincent.

All around her she heard murmurs of "Wonderful! Wonderful!" "Remarkable for such a little girl!" Vincent tossed her head. She was twenty years old, though perhaps tonight in her costume she didn't look more than fifteen.

Somebody brought her a message from a Miss Caroline Dow who wanted to speak to her privately. Norma and Vincent were taken to a more or less secluded corner where Miss Dow and a few of her friends were sitting. They shook hands warmly. Miss Dow questioned Vincent about what she did and what her plans were. She told her about the poems in the St. Nicholas magazine and how she had written poetry from an early age.

Miss Dow took Norma aside and confided, "I'd like to do something for Vincent. Do you think it would be all right if we made up a purse for her? No, I can see that will not do. But I would like to help her realize her talent. I'm certain she can be a great poet."

It was getting late and few of the guests still remained. Vincent and Norma said good-by, but not before Miss Dow had extracted from them the promise that they would see each other again before she returned to New York the following week.

"I'll send a taxi for you tomorrow evening," Miss Dow called after them as they were leaving. "Be sure to bring some of your other poems with you."

Vincent came to see Miss Dow the next night and the next and the next. Then Miss Dow asked her if she could call on her mother.

Caroline Dow had a long talk with Mrs. Millay about Vincent's future. In the end, she suggested that Vincent apply for a scholarship at Vassar College. She promised to attempt to interest some of her friends in Vincent's promising career; they might perhaps be willing to contribute to her expenses at college.

Vincent was aglow with the idea. In her wildest dreams she had never imagined anything like this. It was the most wonderful thing that ever happened to anybody, Vincent thought as she bade Miss Dow good-by.

When "Renascence" was printed in *The Lyric Year* in November, it created a sensation. Many well-known poets— far older than Vincent—found it a remarkable poem. They were indignant that it had not won a prize. The winner of the first prize himself wrote, ". . . when the book arrived I realized that it was an unmerited award. The outstanding poem in that book was 'Renascence' by Edna St. Vincent Millay, immediately acknowledged by every authoritative critic as such. The award was as much an embarrassment to me as a triumph."

In far-off Iowa, two young graduates of Harvard College, Witter Bynner and Arthur Davison Ficke, who were them-selves contributing poets, leafed through the book on Thanksgiving Day and came upon "Renascence." They sat down in the park at the base of the Soldier's Monument and read the poem aloud. They sent a letter to Vincent, saying "This is Thanksgiving Day and we thank you. . . ."

One of them could not believe that a young girl had written such a strong, fresh poem. He wrote to the editor:

> . . . The thing that has moved me, personally, into wanting to write to you is your choice of Miss Millay's poem for the first prize. And the other judges passed it by! . . . We grew somewhat downhearted over most of the poems, . . . including our own. And suddenly we stumbled on this one, which really lights up the whole book. It seems to both of us a real vision. . . . Are you at liberty to name the author? The little item about her in the

back of the book is a marvel of humor. No sweet young thing of twenty ever ended a poem precisely where this one ends: it takes a brawny male of forty-five to do that . . . if it's a real secret we respect the writer of such a poem far too much to want to plague "her."

The editor asked Vincent to drop the two young poets a "line" to thank them for the compliment and at the same time convince them of their error.

Vincent wrote to Mr. Ficke and Mr. Bynner:

Mr. Earle has acquainted me with your wild surmise. Gentlemen: I must convince you of your error; my reputation is at stake. I simply will not be a "brawny male." Not that I have an aversion to brawny males: *au contraire, au contraire*. But I cling to my femininity!

Is it that you consider brain and brawn so inseparable? —I have thought otherwise. Still, that is all a matter of personal opinion. But, gentlemen: when a woman insists that she is twenty you must not call her forty-five. That is more than wicked; it is indiscreet.

Mr. Ficke, you are a lawyer. I am very much afraid of lawyers. Spare me, kind sir! Take into consideration my youth—for I am indeed but twenty—and my fragility—for "I do protest I am a maid"—and—sleuth me no sleuths!

Seriously: I thank you also for the compliment you have unwittingly given me. For tho I do not yet aspire to be forty-five and brawny, if my verse so represents me, I am more gratified than I can say. When I was a little girl, this is what I thought and wrote:

Let me not shout into the world's great ear
Ere I have something for the world to hear.

Then let my message like an arrow dart
And pierce a way into the world's great heart.

You cannot know how much I appreciate what you
have said about my "Renascence."

If you should care to look up the April, 1907, number
of *Current Literature,* you would find a review of my
"Land of Romance" (near a review of Mr. Bynner's
"Fair of my Fancy"). . . .

E. St. V. M.

P.S. The brawny male sends his picture. I *have* to laugh.

THIRTEEN

Vincent was leaving home. At the little railroad station in Rockland the small family group clustered around the vivid figure in green with the fiery red hair. Though she would be twenty-one in less than three weeks, Vincent looked no more than sixteen as she stood there chatting brightly with her mother and two sisters. Mother Millay suppressed a sigh at the thought of her first-born's imminent departure. Nothing must spoil this moment of Vincent's triumph. It was what she had always dreamed for her—for all of them. To leave the narrow little town was the only solution—unless they were to become satisfied with humdrum lives. Mother Millay was glad for Vincent—though it seemed only yesterday she was a tiny child.

Vincent was wholly happy. She was going to New York—not for a short visit and to see the sights—but to live and to go to Barnard College there. Not that she was to be just a college girl like anybody else. Miss Dow had decided that until Vincent could enter Vassar College the following autumn, a semester at Barnard would serve to settle her into a student's pace, for it had been three and a half years since Vincent had attended any school. A number of poets had written to her and wanted to meet her when she came to New York. It was almost as if she were a celebrity. And one boy who had read "Renascence" in *The Lyric Year* had written her from Texas asking for her autograph.

The train whistle blew twice and Vincent swung aboard

with her suitcase. As the train started chugging out, she waved frantically to her mother and Norma and Kathleen. Her face was as flushed as her hair and she was so excited she scarcely knew what she was doing. Imagine—she, E. Vincent Millay—was going to New York to go to college! It was almost as if it were happening to somebody else, for E. Vincent Millay was her professional name. Vincent pinched herself to be sure she was awake and not dreaming. She looked out at the snowy landscape with the snow-tipped evergreen trees that seemed to be moving backward while the train stood still. It was not until they reached Woolwich and the train had to be ferried across the Kennebec River to Bath that she really believed she was on her way.

Cousin George was at the station in Portland to meet her. He carried her suitcase across the glass arcade to the New York train. George smiled indulgently at Vincent as she darted about exclaiming, "Just imagine! I'm going Pullman all the way—and in a lower berth, too. When do I tip the porter? In the morning? And a dime? Right. Now you'd better go, George, or you'll end up in New York with me. Good-by! Good-by! Love to Aunt Susie and Uncle Frank. Quick. The train is moving."

New York was more than Vincent dared expect. To her, the grand canyons of the tall buildings were like fairy castles surrounded by moats of busy city streets. She lived in the heart of it at the residence hall of the Y.W.C.A. Training School at East Fifty-second street, of which Miss Caroline Dow, her benefactor, was executive secretary. Vincent's room was on the eighth floor, where she could look out high over the city. She found the sounds and sights and smells exciting. Her entire life in New York was vastly different from that of Camden. Every morning a maid came to tidy her room. Dinner was at night—at seven o'clock on the eleventh floor —with Vincent sitting at Miss Dow's left at the head table.

During the day Aunt Caroline—as she wanted to be called—was always busy, for her position was an important one and demanding. Almost before she knew what was happening, Vincent, too, had a crowded schedule and was leading a busy life, going to school, attending the theater and concerts, visiting art galleries and being entertained by the great and the near-great of the literary set.

She immediately enrolled in an English course at Barnard, which she attended every morning at ten. It was not long before she was the star of the course, for both the professor and the girls in the class admired and lauded her stories. They had a system of critics for the compositions. A slip of paper was attached to the front page of each piece of work, concealing the name of the author. Then the story or essay or poem was shuffled and passed around and each "critic" could write her comments on the slip of paper. Vincent's work was almost invariably praised. Once, having no original composition to pass in, she fearfully submitted a poem she had already written—"Interim." The professor read it aloud to the class and found it a remarkable poem for a girl in college.

Vincent's social success as a poetess went far beyond the college walls. Sara Teasdale, already well on the way to fame, invited her to tea so they could get to know one another and talk about their poetry. Miss Jessie Rittenhouse, the secretary of the Poetry Society of America, gave a party in Vincent's honor. There Vincent met Witter Bynner, the young poet with whom she had corresponded when he had written to her from Davenport, Iowa, thanking her for "Renascence." Vincent and Witter liked one another immediately and they talked eagerly together for most of the evening. When there was a lull in the conversation, Miss Rittenhouse asked him to read "Renascence" so all the people at the party could hear it again. It was wonderful for Vincent to hear it like this, for Witter had a beautiful voice and he read well. For the first time in her life she had a chance to sit back and be modest. Admired by her peers she could accept their admiration as graciously as it was offered. There was no straining to be the genius, the center of attention, the Bohemian hoyden. At last she could relax and be the nice young girl she was, for no one in New York would be very impressed with her sophistication, she felt, except perhaps Witter Bynner. Drawing out a cigarette case at the party, he asked her if she would mind if he smoked.

Vincent replied, "Not in the least."

At that he offered her a cigarette, which she refused somewhat archly. Raising his eyebrows, Witter said that no doubt she was not a smoker of cigarettes (a daring innovation for a young girl barely out of her teens in 1913). Vincent intimated that her only objection was smoking publicly at a party given in her honor. Witter gave her to understand that he was glad she was not prejudiced against smoking, for his sister had been prejudiced but that now she smoked more than he did.

Vincent felt she had more than vindicated herself in this worldly exchange and was ready for everything New York had to offer. She mingled freely with the rich and the famous, for this young girl from Camden had appeared like a comet on the literary scene. In intellectual circles "Renascence" was beginning to be well known and everyone was interested in its author. In the first flush of discovery, Vincent found life in New York could be wonderful. There was a coterie of young men—college students who had read her poetry and admired it or friends of the poets she had met—who escorted her to the theater and to opera. Everyone seemed to want to do everything they could for her and all the important people she met treated her as an equal, a sort of special equal because she was so young. Even her old love for the theater was completely and wonderfully satisfied when she saw Sarah Bernhardt in *Camille*. She was taken to see the famous International Art Exhibition at the Armory with its sensational cubistic works, and planned to send her family post cards of some of the pictures.

Within two months, *The Forum* magazine bought two of Vincent's poems—"Journey" and "O, World, I Cannot Hold Thee Close Enough." How thrilled she was when she opened the envelope and found a check for twenty-five dollars, instead of a rejection slip or a note full of praise for her work but regretting that the magazine could not accept it for publication. She looked long and hard at the check, hoping that she had broken the jinx of "no profit" at last. Then she endorsed the check and sent it off to her mother, begging her to use the money to make things easier for herself and also to buy one whimsical article for each one of them with what was left—something they did not *need* but could keep as a reminder.

Ten days later, Mitchell Kennerley, owner of *The Forum* and a book publisher, offered to publish a volume of Vincent's poems. After giving the matter some serious thought, Vincent decided against it. She did not believe it would be a wise move, yet. First, she wanted to finish her education and then begin building her reputation as a poetess upon a solid foundation encompassing scholarship as well as inspiration. There was so much she did not yet know. Now that fame was within her grasp, it was easy to push it back for another four years. She wanted to study and learn everything she could and just write poetry until she was sure she could sustain fame. Being known and accepted by the professors and girls at Barnard and the small select circle of poets in New York and the group of patrons who were going to send her through Vassar was enough for the present.

Vincent continued to send single poems to *The Forum*

for publication. In the May, 1913, issue, both her poem "Journey" and Witter Bynner's one-act play on the White Slave Traffic called *Tiger* were published, and that gave her a feeling of companionship—of being in step with the literary tempo of her time. Vincent felt she was moving in just the right circles and at the proper pace. Delight succeeded delight; one wonderful sensation after another came to her in New York. She was exactly in the center of things, where she had always wanted to be, and she was supremely happy.

For scarcely more than four months Vincent enjoyed New York to the hilt. Life had never been fuller or more exciting. Then at the end of the semester, her course in English 24 at Barnard finished with flying honors, Vincent went home to Camden for the summer. In the fall she was to enter Vassar and there was a summer of hard study before her. Elizabeth E. Haight, the professor of Latin at Vassar, tutored her in that subject by mail. Vincent also had to take examinations in mathematics and American history. Her old enemy algebra stood in the way, and she said all she knew about American history was one verse of "The Star-Spangled Banner." But she studied these by herself and entered Vassar that autumn when she was well past twenty-one.

Vincent had so looked forward to going to Vassar. She daydreamed about it all summer long as she paddled her canoe across Megunticook Lake. The girls would be so wonderful. She had looked them up in the catalogue and there were four girls from Persia, two from Syria, two from Japan, one from India, one from Berlin, Germany, and one or two others from across the sea. It would be such fun to know them.

When she arrived at Vassar she was just another freshman. Professor Haight came to meet her but nobody else paid much attention to her. Vincent felt self-conscious because she was at least three or four years older than the rest of the girls in her class and she had to obey the same rules. They were supposed to be in their own dormitories every night at a childishly early hour, and the house mother checked on them. On Saturday night they were permitted to stay out later, but they had to sign out, saying where they were going, and sign in again. In addition to this, she was taking fifteen hours of classwork in required subjects. Gone was her freedom, her independence. They were trying to transform her into a tame, well-behaved little schoolgirl—and she had never been that.

It was particularly hard for her because of the taste of cosmopolitan life she had enjoyed during her few months in New York. She was disappointed because the campus was not as beautiful as she had imagined—not on the Hudson River at all—nor was college life as amusing as she had thought it would be. After the intellectual stimulation of her circle of friends in New York, she was sure that if *Alice in Wonderland* had had a college, it would have been exactly like Vassar. She railed against the regulations of the authorities. She complained that the college was run like an orphan asylum and its inmates pacified by ice cream and candy. She was a child no longer, she cried, and she wanted to be trusted to make the proper adult decisions.

At first, the college authorities were as unhappy with Vincent as she was with them. She had a schedule of courses, but the professor of the class would never know whether or not she was going to attend. She explained very frankly to them that sometimes it seemed more important to her to write a poem or read something that really interested her.

Gradually Vincent made friends among the girls. She was promoted to a higher class in French and made a member of the French Club, an unusual honor for a freshman. For one of its functions she wrote a poem in French to the tune of "Au Clair de la Lune," in honor of one of the teachers who was leaving for a semester. French was still a favorite subject of hers. Besides French she was studying history, geometry, Latin, German and Old English. Two of them were sophomore courses and by the time the midyear examinations came Vincent felt swamped and studied very hard. She and her friends Kim, Bee and Harry started reading the Bible together in Harry's room, and Vincent discovered for herself its loveliness. By the time spring came Vincent liked Vassar and Vassar had, willy-nilly, become accustomed to her ways. They drew lots for the next year's rooms and she was very happy with hers—a corner room with two windows in the most popular dormitory—with room for all of her things—and there were four of her friends on the floor below.

With characteristic changeability, Vincent had by this time begun to adore everything about Vassar and college life, including her studies and the professors. She had great plans for the following years and nothing could have kept her away from Vassar. By this time, too, she had quite won the hearts of both the girls and the faculty by virtue of her winning personality, her talent, her willingness to participate in any college function where she could be of help, and her very real intellectual capacity. Nothing was too difficult for her to attempt scholastically, and Vassar soon realized that she was a rare and extraordinary student.

As a sophomore at Vassar Vincent began to distinguish herself. The vivid little figure with the bright red hair was becoming a familiar sight on the gray and pink campus. "Interim," the poem which the professor at Barnard had liked so well, won a prize. Vincent joined the Dramatic Club and everybody accorded her acting abilities great respect. In the spring, she played the role of the poet Marchbanks in a production of Shaw's *Candida*. Vincent never thought that *she* would ever play the role of a man on the stage, but that is the way it had to be in a girls' school. All the girls crowded around her and said she was perfect in the part. They thought no one else better deserved to play the role of the poet. Vincent blossomed under their frank adoration and took part in all the activities she could. People asked her to sing and she often gave impromptu concerts, singing her little songs.

She composed the official marching song for the class of 1917—her class. At the Sophomore Tree Ceremonies, the class marched around the campus for hours singing their marching song for the first time. It was a Vassar tradition and the ceremonies were said to be the best they had ever had at the college.

The following autumn was Vassar's fiftieth anniversary. An elaborate celebration was planned well in advance. Before she finished her sophomore year, Vincent knew that she would play the role of Marie de France in Hazel Mac-Kaye's *Pageant of Athera*, a coveted part which she described to her mother as "lovely." And as a junior Vincent did make a lovely princess when she, as Marie de France, addressed the court in the open air theater telling how "The Lay of the Honeysuckle" was written.

It was during her junior year, too, that Vincent's poem "Suicide" was entered in the intercollegiate competition and won the cup for Vassar. This attracted almost as much attention as "Renascence"—especially among the men's colleges. Almost every college boy who wrote poetry himself or was interested in literature began writing to Vincent. There was Harrison Dowd at Andover, who had long been a correspondent of hers. She described him to her sister Norma as a "perfect dear," though she had not yet met him. Edmund Wilson of Princeton knew her poems through his cousin Caroline who was at Vassar. Vincent still corresponded with Arthur Davison Ficke, though they had not yet met. She knew Witter Bynner from her first days in New York. Though they quarreled intermittently, they were close friends. Perhaps Vincent's most exotic correspondent was Salomón de la Selva, a young Nicaraguan poet.

During her senior year at Vassar, Salomón came to the United States to teach Spanish at Williams College. He invited Vincent to spend a week end at Williams as the guest of a colleague of his in the Spanish Department—Professor Rice and his wife. The restrictions at Vassar were somewhat relaxed for seniors—they were allowed to spend week ends off campus with special permission. After some uncertainty, Vincent was finally permitted to go to Williamstown for the last half of the Thanksgiving week end. She loved the blue hills of the Berkshires in the winter. Professor and Mrs. Rice did everything to make her feel welcome and at home. Vincent showed Salomón the three poems that she had sold to *Poetry Magazine* for sixteen dollars—"Kin to Sorrow," "Tavern" and "Afternoon on a Hill." A fourth poem, "October-November" had been rejected because the editor said they would have to wait until the following autumn to print it. Salomón agreed with Vincent that it was stupid. "To print verse in season is as insulting as illustrating it," Vincent pointed out.

Salomón, agreeing, kept saying in obvious admiration, "October-November. October-November—Ah, Ednah!"

The week end at Williams was perfect. There was a concert Saturday night, and on Sunday afternoon Mrs. Taylor, the wife of the head of the Romance Language Department, played Bach, Schumann and Chopin for them. Vincent thought she played almost as well as Paderewski. The perfect week end was over much too soon.

She returned to Vassar moody and impatient. The taste of the adult world made her vaguely dissatisfied. Here she was —almost twenty-five—still a schoolgirl. She had her good friends among the girls at the college. Being so much older, however, she was the leader; they, the followers. Everything came her way now almost too easily. She played the role of Vigdis in John Masefield's *Locked Chest*. Masefield himself wrote her a letter from England saying that a great many of his friends had written to him telling him how wonderful she was and that he wished he could have been there. Vincent sent him some of her poems and he wrote back that she had a "quite rare personal gift." It went without saying that when the senior class produced Vincent's own poetic play "The Princess Marries the Page," she played the leading role.

Vincent was reaching out for life. She tried to go to New York as often as she could to see the latest plays and attend concerts and the opera. She was beginning to think of the future as her last semester at Vassar came to a close. She had already arranged for her sister Kathleen to enter Vassar the next fall. She wanted to get a job in New York and have Norma come and study at the School of Design. And Mother Millay must come, too, just to enjoy New York. Vincent knew she would never make enough money as a poet—for didn't poets always starve?—so she decided to try to find work as an actress.

The last few months at Vassar were pleasant enough, and passed quickly—almost like a dream. Soon it was warm and they were making plans for commencement. Vincent's baccalaureate hymn had been chosen by the class. At the commencement exercises the words of the Tree Ceremonies and the marching song, which Vincent had written as a sophomore, would be repeated and some of her other songs sung. Unlike her high school graduation, where she had to fight tooth and nail for every honor and recognition, everyone at Vassar seemed to want her to have as large a part as possible. It was almost too good to be true. She had only to take her final examinations and then she would be able to sign herself "Edna St. Vincent Millay, A.B."

The weather was so warm and pleasant Vincent was delighted when her roommate Charlotte Babcock invited her to take a two-day motor trip with two other girls. Cars were enough of a novelty in 1917 so that it was an event to ride through the verdant summer landscape for fifty miles. They stayed overnight at the house of one of the girls and the next day had dinner at the home of the other. Vincent enjoyed every moment of it and thought she would remember it all her life as the last perfect week end at Vassar.

Poor absent-minded, careless Vincent. So happy was she with her honors and friends and pleasure in spring, she had forgotten that she had already lost her privileges by staying in New York to go to the opera. As a penalty, the faculty took away her part in the commencement exercises. Vincent wept and wept. She had sat up three nights in a row studying for her final examinations, and she was on the verge of breaking down completely. All the girls were sympathetic and kind.

Charlotte tried to comfort her. "You just wait and see, Vincent," she said. "We'll get up a petition and they'll let you stay for commencement."

"It won't do any good," Vincent intoned dully. "I came in through the back door and that's the way I have to leave, apparently. I can't ever seem to do anything right."

"Now, Vincent, don't say that," Charlotte consoled her. "You've brought more honor to Vassar than any other girl in our class. They'll be sorry someday they did this to you."

Professor Haight came to her room to explain that it was not as bad as it sounded.

"Your part in the commencement will go on without you," she explained. "They'll still sing your baccalaureate hymn and repeat the words of the Tree Ceremonies, and all your songs and the class marching song will grace the final activities."

"But the way they're making me leave the campus is awful," Vincent wailed, "as if I were a leper or something not even fit to be on the same grounds as the graduates. And after all I've done for the college."

"There, there, dear, don't take it so hard. You'll get your diploma all the same through the mail," Miss Haight said as she patted her shoulder.

"Shipped to me like a salted fish," Vincent answered with a sudden flash of spirit. "What can I tell my mother?"

Vincent never knew she had so many friends at Vassar. There was a steady stream of girls in and out of her room, offering indignant sympathy and reporting the latest stratagems they were using on the faculty. "We are making one huge, splendid row," Charlotte told her with satisfaction.

Vincent packed and left immediately as the faculty had ordered her to. She had no sooner explained to Aunt Caroline what had happened when she received a telegram calling her back to Vassar. The class had fought so valiantly for her, and so many people had signed the petition, that the faculty had reconsidered—she would be allowed to come back to the campus and graduate in her cap and gown with the rest.

She almost flew back to Poughkeepsie. The commencement exercises were beautifully done and extraordinarily moving. Vincent was with all her college friends and she left Vassar gloriously happy and victorious.

FOURTEEN

Ever since she was a child, Vincent had known that poets traditionally starved. So it was as an actress that she came back to New York to earn her living after her graduation from college. She had had enough of poverty and cold and meager meals in her youth.

Armed with high courage and a sheaf of introductions to stage managers, Vincent made the rounds of the casting offices. She decided upon Edna Millay as a stage name because it sounded more dignified and feminine. Salomón de la Selva was in New York and he had always preferred to call her Edna, so Edna she became. Disappointment followed disappointment. She did not get the Milwaukee season for eight weeks in the summer, which had been mentioned as a possible opening for her. The producer of a hit play on Broadway would have given her a secondary part in his new play, but her hair was too near the color of the leading lady's.

It was Professor Haight who came to Vincent's rescue and arranged some poetry readings for her at the home of Mrs. Hooker, a wealthy friend. Vincent's trunk had not come, so she wore a gown of Mrs. Hooker's for the occasion. The borrowed dress had a train and, being too large, it hung about six inches on the floor around her. However, since it was made of three rainbow-colored scarves, the audience did not notice anything wrong and probably considered it extremely artistic. Vincent was an immediate success and was asked to do several other readings later in the week. Edith Wynne Matthison, another friend, obtained an engagement for her at the Bennet School near Vassar, and Vincent was launched on her new career.

To live up to their conception of the ethereal appearance of a young poetess, Vincent decided she must have long, trailing dresses. She appealed to Norma, who had always been extremely gifted with her hands, to concoct a garment, graceful and delicately colored, from some chiffon scarves they had at home. Throughout most of her life, Vincent continued this career that she had entered so light-heartedly and unexpectedly. In later years she was able to earn a great deal of money but always—whether the monetary reward was large or small—she tried to look like a poetess should and read her work with its full measure of beauty and sonority.

Although the theatrical business was not booming for Vincent, the poetry readings made her feel better because she was earning some money, and reciting to an audience was somewhat related to the theater. Most important of all, she had finally agreed to have her first book of poems published by Mitchell Kennerley. It was going to be printed on expensive, deckle-edged paper and bound in black with gold letters. It would be a thin book—beautifully designed—as perfect as any girl could want for her first book of poems. She felt thrilled and humble all at once when she saw the title page with her own name on it—stark and lonesome with so much white space around it. Now with her work between the hard covers of a book, she was joining the company of all authors who had preceded her. There was something so permanent about a book. It was not an object easily discarded like last month's magazine or yesterday's newspaper. People kept books on the shelves of their homes and libraries for years. Though many of the poems had been printed before and "Renascence," the poem which gave the book its title, had appeared between hard covers with ninety-nine other poems, an entire book of her poems alone was wholly different and a little frightening. Critics would review it and only she was responsible for each page of its contents.

But Vincent wanted Norma with her and shortly before Thanksgiving, she sent her twenty-five dollars with which to come to New York. She hoped that perhaps by the following Thanksgiving she might be able to send for Mother Millay and reunite the family. For New York was Vincent's town—a great and fabulous city in which she was beginning to feel completely at home. Gaily dressed in a wisteria velvet skirt and green blouse, she roamed the city with her friends, meeting people uptown whom she knew downtown, thrilled by each unexpected encounter. She lived in Greenwich Village, but she was not quite of it. Her wealthy friends, who had underwritten her college career at Vassar, surrounded her with friendship and admiration— often inviting her to share the rich luxury of their surroundings. When she at last met Harrison Dowd after corresponding with him throughout college, he asked her with a certain shyness, "How does it feel to be a success?" He fell in love with her as did Edmund Wilson, an aspiring poet and littérateur, John Peale Bishop, his friend, and a host of other young men. Salomón de la Selva was living in New York now, and Vincent saw him frequently, dining with him at the better restaurants and drawing him into her circle of friends. Some of the young men who were in love with Vincent wanted to marry her, but she was not yet ready to settle down.

When Norma arrived in New York, they found a small room in the heart of Greenwich Village at 139 Waverly Place. A few blocks away on MacDougal Street, the Provincetown Players were starting their venture. They advertised for a girl to play the ingenue part in *The Angel Intrudes*. Vincent, slender and small with red-gold hair, answered the call and presented herself at the greenroom over the stable to read the lines of Annabelle. Floyd Dell, the author of the play, thought she looked the part and acted it competently, so he hired her at once, though the company paid no salaries. As she was leaving she wrote down her name as "Edna Millay," and he wondered whether she was Edna St. Vincent Millay who had written the astonishing "Renascence" which he, as well as the entire company, had read and found so marvelous.

Both Norma and Vincent acted with the Provincetown Players, receiving their reward in satisfaction and accolades but no money. They became poorer and poorer as the winter grew colder. They were acting in the theater, busy with their roles, as they wanted to be, but there were days when they had nothing but bread and tea. Still, they were happy.

In addition to acting, Vincent wrote a good deal, for she felt she was really living. Norma, with her remarkably clever fingers, made hats and sometimes was fortunate enough to sell them. World War I was raging and Norma found work in a defense plant that made airplanes. Although Vincent was not strong enough for heavy work, she tried to make her contribution in other ways. She became something of a pacifist, for the war had turned her thoughts to the needless slaughter of young boys and men, and she soon perceived that their deaths had not "saved the world for democracy." Soon after the war she wrote an inspired play called *Aria da Capo*. She herself considered it one of the best things she had ever written. The Provincetown Players accepted it for performance as an important antiwar play. Vincent directed it and Norma and Harrison Dowd played the leading roles of Columbine and Pierrot. A young artist named Charles Ellis designed the costumes and settings and played the role of one of the shepherds. The second shepherd was James Light and Hugh Ferris, another artist, played Cothurnus. *Aria da Capo* became a classic theater piece of its kind, and is still performed by college groups. In honor of Norma's part in the play, Vincent wrote the spritely Columbine sonnet. Norma's passion for the theater continued and she went on to become a good professional actress, eventually graduating to parts in Broadway shows. Vincent, however, began losing interest in acting as such, especially since she was not paid for it, and devoted more time to her writing.

By the following Thanksgiving Vincent was trying to find ways and means to bring her mother to New York. She still did not have very much money, but she was now writing magazine pieces under the name of Nancy Boyd and selling them. Salomón de la Selva had gone off to London and she often thought of how they used to ride back and forth on the ferry, a merry pastime which she missed. Allan Ross MacDougall went off to Europe, soon to be followed by Harrison Dowd and a host of other friends. Witter Bynner and Arthur Davison Ficke sailed for the Orient.

Vincent was busy working on a second book of poems which she hoped Mitchell Kennerley would publish in the fall. Mother Millay came to New York and the three Millays lived in an unfashionable, uncomfortable apartment on West Nineteenth Street, way over near the docks. In her bright clothes, Vincent was a picturesque figure as she emerged from the old tenement house. The children on the street swarmed about her and she often gave them rides in her taxi for a few blocks before going on to her destination. When Vincent sold a story she scattered her money around with prodigious ease, treating her mother and Norma to dinners at the Brevoort and other expensive restaurants, and then, all too soon, there was none. But that was Vincent and Vincent's way and nothing could change her. The magazines which printed her stories offered her more money if she would sign "Edna St. Vincent Millay" to them rather than Nancy Boyd, but she wanted to reserve her own name for her serious poetic work of which she was truly proud. Her acting and her beautiful poetry had made her the darling of Greenwich Village. She still worked very hard and conscientiously at her poems and though they were bringing her fame—lasting fame, she hoped—she still could not earn enough money from them to support herself and her mother, to do nice things for Norma and to help Kathleen at Vassar.

When spring came, she was tired of the dirt and noise of the city. She sold a short story for four hundred dollars under her assumed name and a moving picture company began negotiating with her for it. With this money which, in any event, would not go far or last long in New York, Vincent determined to take her entire family on a long summer vacation of at least five months—possibly six. The four of them were together again and they found a ramshackle little house on a windy hill in Truro on Cape Cod. It was only nine miles from Provincetown where the Provincetown Players had their inception and were now playing. Norma was intensely interested in acting. Vincent could work on her poems. The wind blew about the cottage continuously and the air was fragrant with pine from the woods behind the house. There was a lonely beach and from the dunes the sandpipers and whippoorwills sang all night long.

There were not many conveniences in the little house, but they practically lived out of doors, swimming, picking berries, eating, sleeping and working as they pleased. Though not one of them knew it, it was the last time in their lives that the four Millays would live together as a family in a little house like the one in Camden by the brook. Vincent wrote a number of poems inspired by their summer on Cape Cod—about the lonesome beach and the sea and the single feather of a gull drifting in the air.

Their friends came to see them. Norma, pretty as a picture and in glowing health, was beginning to be seriously interested in Charles Ellis. All the actors of the Provincetown Players were frequent visitors at the little house, and there were many gay evenings when they played Beethoven's *Fifth Symphony* on their borrowed Victrola or strummed tunes and sang far into the night. Kathleen met a young playwright who seemed to like her a great deal. Edmund Wilson, an ardent admirer of Vincent's, came to Cape Cod. He asked Vincent to marry him and she said she would think about it. Perhaps he would be the solution. But a few weeks later Vincent went to Woodstock, New York, for a visit and there she met a handsome Italian singer from the Metropolitan Opera Company. His name was Luigi Mario Laurenti and they became friends. In a way he took the place of Salomón de la Selva. Vincent began learning Italian, and that seemed the important part of the friendship to her. All thoughts of marriage to Wilson fled for the time being.

When the winds started blowing cold about their little cottage on the hill, the Millays departed. Kathleen returned to Vassar and her studies. Mother Millay decided that New York was not for her and went back to Newburyport for the winter. Norma was planning her marriage to Charles Ellis, so Vincent took a large room for herself at 77 West Twelfth Street in the nicest part of Greenwich Village. It was expensive and she did not quite know how she was to pay for it with her spasmodic earnings, but she was determined to make a home for herself there. She decorated it in Chinese style with teakwood tables and Oriental screens in honor of Witter Bynner and Arthur Davison Ficke, who were in the Orient. She missed them very much and it made her feel closer to them.

She won a prize of one hundred dollars for her "Beanstalk" poem and spent it all on clothes. She bought a new evening gown and shoes to go with it, and also stockings with embroidery up the front. She saw a gorgeous red dress she would have liked to buy, but she could never wear red on account of her hair. For good measure, she had her beautiful red hair cut in a modern bob. It took all the courage she had to do it, but once her decision was made and the deed done she felt like a newly emancipated woman. No more long sessions of brushing and pinning and arranging that waist-length mane of hair before the mirror. A lick and a promise, a flick of the comb—and she was ready now to face all comers.

If Vincent's second book of poems *Second April* had come out on schedule, she would have been happy. By November it had still not appeared, and she wished she had listened to Witter Bynner when he advised her against publishing with Mitchell Kennerley. The delay was making her miserable.

From the high elation of finding a nice place to live, decorating it, bobbing her hair, winning the poetry prize and spending it all on clothes, her mood gave way to despair. She contracted bronchitis and was too ill to work. The bills piled up and were left unpaid. Kathleen suddenly married Howard Irving Young, the playwright, and left Vassar in her third year. Vincent felt old—and she was not progressing at all with her poetry.

In the midst of all this, the editor of *Vanity Fair* offered her a position as foreign correspondent for the magazine. It entailed going to Europe and sending back two articles a month—one under her own name and the other signed Nancy Boyd. To Vincent, the offer seemed a godsend. Fresh scenes and sensations for her eyes and mind to feast upon— time to work and be alone—and no money worries. She made her decision quickly, for now she was not sorry to be leaving New York.

FIFTEEN

There was a gay *bon voyage* party in Vincent's stateroom aboard the French liner *Le Rochambeau* the gray January day she sailed for Europe. Vincent's neatly clipped red head bobbed here and there among the people who had come to say good-by. With all her pretty new clothes—and the great white Hudson Bay blanket and new dark-blue silk umbrella that were parting gifts—there was scarcely room for them all in the tiny cabin and they overflowed into the corridor. The little bandbox bellboys in their pert uniforms hurried in and out with extra chairs and glasses—speaking French. It was like being in France. All the toasts were drunk from champagne glasses and proposed in French. Then the steamship whistles blew insistently and the guests were hurried off the boat. Vincent waved to her friends and her sisters and brother-in-law as long as she could see them, muttering under her breath, *"Au revoir, mes amis, au revoir."* Then she turned her attention to Manhattan's receding sky line. Never had it looked so beautifully fairylike as now when she was leaving it.

Then came complete relaxation. She had been tensely keyed up for a week—getting ready and packing her clothes and seeing to a thousand and one things. Nothing back there or what lay before her in Europe would matter for the next nine days. The ship was a world isolated in itself. Vincent changed her clothes three times a day, spoke French constantly, ate frogs legs and snails, had baked Alaska for dessert

and drank white wine with all her meals except breakfast.
Fortunately, she was a good sailor, for the winter voyage was
rough and stormy and nearly everybody else was seasick. On
the ninth day of the trip, Vincent could not sleep for excitement. She finally dressed at six o'clock in the morning and
went up on the wet, slippery deck to see the sun rise over
France. The sun didn't come out that day since it was rain-
ing, but she was thrilled all the same at being between the
coast of Cornwall and Brittany. It made her think of Tristan
and Isolde and their sad love story. And soon she would be
in Paris—the city of her dreams—just as she had imagined
she would be one day back in high school in Camden, Maine.

She was thrilled by Paris. Every morning at the Hotel des
Saints Pères a maid, who spoke only French, brought her a
breakfast of rich hot chocolate and brioche—crescent-shaped
rolls—with tiny curls of sweet butter and jam, while she was
still in bed. In her lovely quilted bed jacket Vincent stretched
luxuriously under the warm covers and thought, What a
lovely way to start the day! If the morning was chilly, the
maid started a fire in the little grate inside the fireplace, and
Vincent arose in a warm glow. She toasted her toes for a
while and then started to work, for as she had written her
mother she was going to Europe as a businesswoman—and
because she wanted to travel. She wrote her articles for
Vanity Fair—her impressions of shipboard life and Europe
and Europeans. She had so many ideas that she didn't quite
know where to begin.

As she had predicted, the change was good for her poetry
and she wrote a new poem—one of her best in quite a while.
Nearly every afternoon Vincent roamed about Paris. It was
a fascinating city with its broad avenues lined with grand
shops and cafés, its narrow, winding streets, its beautiful
cathedrals centuries old, its palaces, museums and parks.
Vincent walked for miles along the Seine, browsing among

the book stalls—to Notre Dame—to the Louvre—through the Tuilleries. Once started, she could not seem to stop. She walked until she was exhausted and then she hailed one of the queer French taxis and rode back to the Hotel des Saints Pères.

Spring in Paris was incredibly beautiful. The chestnut trees bloomed like candelabra along the Seine, the Bois de Bologne turned a lush green, and Punch and Judy shows were given for children in all the parks. Friends began to filter into Paris. Allan Macdougall was there editing a column for the Paris edition of the Chicago *Tribune*. Harrison Dowd came from Berlin, where he had been playing the piano in a jazz band, and Edmund Wilson was at a hotel just around the corner. It was warm enough to sit out of doors at the sidewalk cafés and drink wine and watch the world go by. Tiny girls came by selling bunches of old-fashioned pinks from baskets they carried on their arms. Vincent sometimes bought a small bouquet, and even sent one flower to her mother, hoping it would retain its fragrance on its journey across the ocean.

Jazz parties were the vogue. One night some visiting Americans, slightly younger than Vincent, invited her to drive with them to the Acacias, a well-known night club with a good jazz band. Pete Chambers asked Vincent's friend Starkie if she could dance.

Starkie answered that he didn't think she could and if she did, she was probably a terrible dancer. He begged Pete to dance with her because he led better. He himself was afraid to try it.

Vincent suspected something of the sort, and when Pete asked her somewhat reluctantly to dance, she outdid herself. Never had she danced more beautifully. A stupid expression came over Pete's face and then he began to enjoy himself. They danced and danced, and Pete went around to everybody in the party telling them, "Vince is wonderful!" Then everybody wanted to dance with Vincent, though they had stood a little in awe of her before because she was a poet and a writer.

In the summertime Vincent went to the French seashore with a party of writers and artists whom she had met in Paris. They took rooms at the Châlet du Nord, at Pourville in Dieppe, and it was like a merry houseparty. Vincent's room looked out over the blue sea. She basked in the sunshine and sand and became freckled and brown. Everyone else stayed only through the month of August, but Vincent liked it so well that she decided to stay on, although only one other girl from England still remained. Judy, the English girl, and Vincent both thought it shameful to leave while the weather was still so grand. When all the other visitors had gone, the Châlet closed and the two of them moved to a small French inn called *Les Algues*.

After the crowd left, they stayed outdoors most of the day, picking berries and wild flowers. There were ripe thickets of blackberry bushes overhanging the bluffs of the sea and lining the roads. Vincent and Judy had the delicious berries all to themselves, for the French considered them poisonous. They literally ate bushels of them, enjoying every morsel. Vincent was fascinated by the wild flowers of the country and determined to learn the names of all the ones she did not already know. Nearly all of them were new to her, though she had encountered a few in the United States under different names. She knew some of the names from literature and poetry, although she had never seen the actual flowers. One day a man named fifty-four of the wild flowers for Vincent while she tried to memorize them. A favorite sight of hers was a field filled with thousands of red poppies, which grew wild in huge drifts around the wheat fields.

On another day Vincent and Judy took a trip to Rouen,

the ancient town where Joan of Arc was kept in prison and then burned at the stake. They visited the tower in which Joan had been a prisoner and later saw the shrine in her honor at the beautiful cathedral of Rouen. Vincent found the old town charming, though the fate of St. Joan made her shiver a bit.

Soon the chill of autumn was in the air and it was time to leave France.

On the stormiest day of the year, the two girls went to Dieppe and crossed the Channel in a tiny steamer to England. They were drenched for the three hours it took to cross but they did not dare go inside the cabin for fear of becoming seasick. One day, they bicycled twenty-five miles to Cambridge and came back by train. Here Vincent received the reviews of her book *Second April,* which Mitchell Kennerley had finally published about a year behind schedule. The reviews were good, but Vincent thought they were better than the book deserved. She resolved to make her next book of poems much better. She began working on her poetry more intensively now, for she had determined to let it rest for a year, and the year was almost up. She felt her poetry had improved, that it was deeper and had more feeling, and it made her happy.

From England she traveled to Rome to visit her friend Richard Washburn Child. In addition to being a writer, he was then the American Ambassador to Italy. When Vincent arrived in Rome Mr. Child suggested that if she really wanted to visit an unusual country, she ought to see Albania and Montenegro before winter set in. John Carter, who worked at the Embassy, made the trip with her. It was the most thrilling experience in her travels in spite of the hardships. There were no railroads or buses of any kind. With few exceptions, there were no roads except for a kind of bridle path through the mountains. Vincent and John traveled by horseback through the mountain passes with an interpreter who spoke no English. He did, however, speak very good Italian which John could understand. The man who owned the horses traveled with them and rode on top of the pack on his horse, rocking back and forth. Two guards, their rifles held in readiness, rode with them because an Albanian had been shot in a feud on this trail the day before.

The first day they rode through the mountains from Tirana to Elbanan in Albania. Although she had been on a horse only once before in her life—and then for just half an hour —she was in the saddle for ten hours. For ten days, twelve or fourteen hours at a stretch, they rode through the mountain passes, starting out before dawn under the moon and the morning star, and arriving at their destination in the evening starlight. Vincent enjoyed every minute of the trip despite the hardships and the inconveniences of traveling in a country where the hotels had fleas but no plumbing, and only sweet, syrupy Turkish coffee. She was entranced with the charming country people in their quaint native costumes and the laughing children they met on the way. Her spirit burgeoned with the lovely, delicately tinted mountain sunrise and the spectacular sunsets.

Their romantic journey on horseback ended when they left their guide, interpreter and guards and crossed the lake of Scutari to Rieca in Montenegro. Part of the boat trip was up a river shut in on both sides by high cliffs and they would have been quite happy except for the racket made by a group of Serbian soldiers on board who spent most of the day shooting at wild ducks. Half deafened and huddled together in a corner of the boat, John Carter and Vincent were fortunate to arrive at Rieca at the end of the day with no bullet holes in them. There they hired an open carriage, drawn by two horses and driven by a elderly, white-bearded Montenegran, to take them to the capital city of Cetinje. They drove over a smooth white road cut for miles along the face of the mountains, ten thousand feet above sea level. To catch a glimpse of occasional isolated farms and sparse gardens, they had to look down a great distance in the growing darkness.

The next day they went on by car to Cattaro, the seaport town where they were to take the boat back to Italy. This ride was the most thrilling experience Vincent had, coming as it did at the end of such an unusual trip through a little-known country. It was over a road much like the one they had traveled the night before, but it was made up entirely of hairpin curves. They traveled at about forty miles an hour, which was considered a good speed in the early twenties. As they were racing along, something was hurled into the car from the road, and the man beside Vincent picked it up and handed it to her with a bow. It was a nosegay of lavender flowers—the "lulet" which she had seen all during the trip through Albania and wanted to pick but hadn't been able to alight from her horse. Now an unknown child by the wayside had tossed it to her just as she was leaving. There could not have been a more touching farewell to any romantic journey.

Back in Rome, Vincent moved into the luxurious Palace Hotel. There she learned that Norma had at last married Charles Ellis. Now both her younger sisters were married. She was glad for Norma and Charles. They had known each other a long time, and Vincent had always thought he would be "the one."

She began to wonder about her own life and her own future. In less than three months she would be thirty and she still was not married. John Carter was due to go home on the twentieth of the month and there was no line of importunate suitors in Europe as there had been in New York. While she was mulling about her future, she lived so extravagantly in Rome—besides going on a shopping spree to console herself—that she soon ran out of money. She had to move to an inexpensive hotel in Vienna, which was then considered the cheapest place for an American to live in Europe. She hated Vienna. The food was incredibly bad and didn't agree with her. There were street riots and generally unsettled conditions, but she felt she had to stay there for a few months to recoup her finances.

Arthur Ficke wrote Vincent that Witter Bynner had sent her a letter asking her to marry him. She had never received it, and all she knew about it was in the postscript of Arthur's letter. The more she thought of the proposal, the more she liked the idea of marrying Witter Bynner. He was a poet, too, and they had a community of interests. While Vincent was living through this difficult and depressing period in Vienna, she decided that if Witter came to Europe sometime in the spring they could decide then if they would marry.

In the meantime she complained that the German food was on the verge of destroying her—it was so heavy with hot breads and boiled cabbage soaked in grease; she would have been happy with an apple. Worst of all she was not getting much work done.

Arthur Ficke rescued Vincent from her misery—much against her will—by sending her a check from his father. It enabled her to leave gray Vienna without any regrets. Vincent celebrated her thirtieth birthday in her small but costly apartment in Budapest, looking out upon the Danube and not quite knowing whether or not she was engaged to Witter Bynner. Her spirits rose in the colorful, gay setting. There was gypsy music in Hungary and all kinds of exotic spiced food, and she received a check for five hundred dollars as an advance on a novel she wanted to write. It made her feel confident and almost incredibly rich and competent.

She suddenly decided that her mother's coming to Europe

—a project which had been delayed several times—was the most important thing in her life just now—even more important than possibly marrying Witter Bynner in the spring. She sent her mother four hundred dollars, and before the end of April Vincent was sitting at a little sidewalk café in the Latin Quarter of Paris with her mother. Mrs. Millay had a cold, the weather was miserable, Vincent had been sick from all the bad food she had eaten, but they were having a grand reunion and a good time. Mother Millay found a little grocery store and bought fruit and dates, crackers and cheese, and they tried to eat a few meals sensibly in their rooms. Mother Millay insisted on seeing every bit of Paris and tried to compress several months of sight-seeing into seven or eight weeks. She went to all Vincent's parties— some that lasted all night or several days—and kept up with the young people.

Vincent and her mother later crossed the Channel to spend the summer in England. They lived in a little house with a thatched roof in the village of Shillingstone in Dorset. Vincent had a separate hut in a pasture where she could be by herself all day. Sometimes a shepherd passed by and grazed his flock of sheep outside her hut. The field had just been mown and the cut grass smelled sweet, and cows and sometimes a horse or two lingered sociably in the doorway, munching the new-mown grass. The hut itself was white-washed inside and had clean straw on the floor. There was a table and a chair and a rope hammock. It was quiet and peaceful and a good place to work, and Vincent went there every morning. Her mother brought lunch to the hut—home-cooked meat, baked potatoes, salad, bread pudding and prunes with cream and milk—and Vincent gradually began to feel better and regained her health.

Every day they went for a long walk, climbing about on the downs or visiting some picturesque little village near by.

Once they walked to Romsey Hants in Hampshire, where one of their ancestors was buried. It was another one of Vincent's dreams come true—a prediction that she had made long ago when she was a child in Camden.

There were lovely birds in England at this season, and Vincent cried the first time she heard a lark's song. She had always been unusually moved by birds in flight and by the music of their singing. But never had she been so touched as at the sight of this drab little brown bird flying straight from the plowed ground, where it nested, high into the air and trilling its joyous song. From this experience Vincent later wrote one of her most beautiful poems called "On First Having Heard the Skylark."

One rainy day she was in Cambridge and saw A. E. Housman, whom she admired for having written *A Shropshire Lad*. She followed his tall, thin figure for about half a mile through the streets until he turned in at Trinity College and disappeared in the dusk. She caught just a glimpse of his face and thought it nice. She had heard that none of the poets in England ever saw him, for he led a shadowy existence, so she considered it quite a triumph to have actually seen something of him. Without her knowing it, A. E. Housman was one of the admirers of Edna St. Vincent Millay's poetry. Her poetry was beginning to be known in England, and enough interest had been shown in it so that some English publishers were planning to bring out a volume of her selected poems. She was thrilled at the thought of being published in London.

The weather was beautiful in Dorset and Vincent and Mother Millay stayed through October and November and then followed the climate and sun to the balmy shores of the French Riviera at Cassis-sur-Mer, Bouches du Rhone. Vincent became very ill once more and some of her friends urged her to come home.

She wanted to return to the United States, but her first concern was to become well again, and one day she almost miraculously recovered her health. It was a day Vincent remembered all her life and looked back upon often, for that day she went swimming in the Mediterranean, from the beach at Cassis, feeling entirely free of pain, and afterward she and her mother walked through the vineyards.

During her days in Europe, Vincent had been trying to make up her mind whether or not to marry Witter Bynner. Before she left for home she already knew she would not.

SIXTEEN

Vincent returned to New York early in 1923, glad to have been in Europe the past two years and just as glad to be back home. Though she was not feeling well and had not written anything for many months and was already past thirty-one, better times were ahead of her. She was still very popular and had a host of friends—both men and women of all ages. Some of her suitors had married and the line had thinned perceptibly. But new friends came her way.

When the Pulitzer awards were announced, Vincent was among the prize winners. Her volume of poems *The Ballad of the Harp Weaver and Other Poems* was judged the best book by an American poet for the year. It was a great honor and signal recognition for the tiny slip of a girl with her bobbed red hair and green eyes. For a poet of such stature, she was incredibly young and she looked no more than barely out of her teens. Her eyebrows—or rather her lack of eyebrows, for they were so light they were practically invisible—gave her a wide-eyed look of innocence that added to the impression that she was a sort of youthful sprite—not earthbound. There was a round of dinners and parties in her honor, her picture was in the newspapers, and she was interviewed and publicized from one end of the country to the other.

Worn out with the excitement and strain of city life after her sudden plunge to public fame, Vincent was glad to slip away to the near-by countryside in May. In the springtime she invariably began to feel restless in New York, and the invitation to be a house guest at Mount Airy in Croton on Hudson came like a godsend. Croton was a lovely village in a scenic section of the valley where writers and artists had bought homes. The sun was warm, the brown earth was slowly turning green and new life was pulsating with the coming of spring and summer. Vincent felt free and happy. Life was good and it was easy to forget one's ills. When she tired of being alone out of doors with the birds and the creatures of the field, there were always delightful people to be found. In the evenings the writers and artists visited at each other's homes and provided their own entertainment—singing or making music or playing games. Their pleasures were simple.

One night while playing charades, Vincent drew as her partner Eugen Boissevain. She had known him casually for a long time. He was a tall, handsome man—an older man who before had always seemed to regard Vincent as a mere child. Playing charades with him as her partner, acting out the characters they had chosen to portray, Vincent noticed for the first time how witty and charming, how subtle and vital he was at close range. She had known him only from a distance, it seemed, and was seeing him for the first time that night. She felt her head swim; she was delightfully happy and confused all at once, but she didn't feel like an awkward little girl in his presence any more. It seemed to Vincent that he was attentive and tender toward her, too, but she couldn't really tell and it didn't matter at all when his clear blue eyes looked into hers. When their part in the charades was over—amid good-natured laughter and derision, everyone assured them that it was a great triumph—Vincent turned toward Eugen and could see that he beamed approval at her. When he asked if he could see her home, she was completely happy. She went to get her coat and overheard two women gossiping in the bedroom.

"Did you ever see two people fall so helplessly in love with each other before a roomful of people?" one observed lightly to the other.

The second woman laughed and said, "I think I know who you mean. Do you suppose anything will come of it?"

Vincent left hurriedly so she would not be caught eavesdropping. She wondered who they could mean, and then realized that they meant her. So this was what was called "falling in love." She had never felt this way before about anybody—happy and protected and secure. She would love him so much that he would simply have to love her in return. She went happily to meet Eugen Boissevain who was to take her home.

She saw Eugen every day. Together they went for long walks and explored the fields and the forests. Eugen had a car—a huge Mercer—and they rode far along the river and up into the mountains and watched the moon rise. At the end of three weeks of fun and happy companionship, Eugen took Vincent's tiny hand in his and asked, "Will you marry me?"

"Yes," Vincent replied gravely. She had known since the night of the charades that she wanted to marry him. There were no doubts or hesitation, obstacles or complications. Everything and everyone else was forgotten.

They planned to be married during the summer. Eugen was worried about Vincent's health—she tired easily and often looked wan—and he insisted on taking her to New York to see a good doctor.

"You must get well, Vincent," he told her with his slight, funny Dutch accent.

So Vincent went to six doctors and was X-rayed and examined and nodded over gravely. She was glad to be doing it at last; except for that one day at Cassis she hadn't felt right for two years. A sensible, practical person, one more concerned about her physical well-being than Vincent, would have done it long ago. The doctor's decision was that she needed an operation and the date was set for July 18.

On the morning of July 18, 1923, Edna St. Vincent Millay and Eugen Boissevain were married at Croton on Hudson. The ceremony took place under the trees outside Eugen's house. Only Norma and her husband Charles and a few close friends were there. At the last moment they decided to dress Vincent like a bride. Eugen wanted it. Strangely enough Vincent, too, found herself longing very much to be married in white, wearing a misty veil and long train. They hurriedly took the white netting which kept out the mosquitoes from the side porch, and Norma, with her deft fingers and experience in theatrical costuming, skillfully draped the yards and yards of diaphanous material about her sister's happy, flushed face and picked white roses from the garden to make a wreath for her head. The train was spread out on the lawn in a long oval. Standing there against the green of the trees and the grass, Vincent was a beautiful bride.

Eugen had not had time to buy a wedding ring. The decision to marry that day had been sudden, for he could not bear the thought of Vincent's facing the ordeal of the operation alone. He borrowed a ring from Hattie, his cook and maid of all work, and slipped it onto the finger of a radiant Vincent when the justice of the peace, whom he had hurriedly summoned from town, pronounced the solemn words. Everyone was gay and merry; only Hattie cried during the ceremony and kept dabbing her eyes intermittently as she served the wedding breakfast. Her Mr. Eugen was married again at last to this beautiful, tiny girl—so different from Inez, his first wife, who had been tall and blond and had died so young. She so hoped Mr. Eugen and his bride would be happy. They both deserved it so.

The wedding guests waved Eugen and Vincent off as they drove away to New York, and later that day Vincent entered a New York hospital for the operation for which arrangements had been previously made.

SEVENTEEN

Vincent awoke in the hospital room wan and tired and so surprised to be alive that it was almost like being born again. She wiggled a toe and spread her fingers before her face. A new life was waiting for her and, she suddenly remembered, she had a new name, too—Mrs. Eugen Boissevain.

"That's fine. You're going to be just fine," said the cheery voice of the doctor. "You'll soon be as good as new."

"Thank you for saving my life, Doctor," Vincent said weakly.

"Don't thank me, thank your husband," boomed the doctor. "If he hadn't brought you in when he did, there's no telling what might have happened."

Eugen was smiling apprehensively at Vincent from the foot of the bed. He came forward to pat her head and hold her hand, but he didn't say a word. Vincent smiled back at him tremulously, feeling safe and secure and cared for as she never had before.

"A bad beginning means a good ending," she observed lightly. Soon it was time for Vincent to rest. Everybody left her bedside as she sank once again into a deep, grateful sleep.

When Vincent recovered, her husband took her back to his house at Croton on Hudson to convalesce. There she lay in the summer sun and read the mail from her friends and sorted the fifty different weeds and shrubs that Esther Root, whom Vincent had first met in Europe, had sent her from Maine, while Eugen commuted to New York to carry on his coffee-importing business. In the fall they would start looking for a house of their own in New York.

As soon as she saw it, Vincent fell in love with the little house on Bedford Street. It was on a quiet, narrow street in Greenwich Village and the main entrance was in a garden which could be reached only by going through a side gate and down a few steps to a brick courtyard—then up a few steps to the garden. The house was only nine and a half feet wide and had two tiny rooms on each of its three floors—but there was a wood-burning fireplace in each room. Across the garden was the Cherry Lane Theater and in the bend of the street an old tavern.

Vincent regarded Eugen, tall and handsome and serious, and wondered if he liked the house as much as she did. The tiny rooms suited Vincent, for she was small, but could a man as tall as Eugen feel at home here? Vincent looked up at his height with questioning eyes.

Eugen squeezed her hand and said, as he bent his head slightly to go through the door, "This is your house, my dear. If you want it, it shall be yours."

"But isn't it too small for you?" Vincent asked in a tiny voice, hoping that it wasn't.

Eugen threw back his head and laughed. "No, no," he protested, "I can fit in. I spend most of the day at the office, anyway, and this will be like coming home to a dollhouse."

Vincent was delighted. "Let's take it! We'll have so much fun fixing it up, and I can have people in for tea before a blazing fire. There'll be room for all our books, and a separate room for poetry. I know we'll be happy here. We can see the snow in winter, and the trees and grass in the spring. It's such a darling little house."

Vincent peered out of the window into the garden. Some

children from a neighboring house were playing with a white cat. Everything seemed perfect.

They moved into the house on New Year's Day. It had been freshly painted and renovated, and Vincent had great fun deciding where all the new furniture and dishes and linens should go. She flew about like a bright-colored hummingbird in her bottle green woolen dress—her neat red head shaking with emphasis as she directed the placing of a desk, a table and a chair. When everything was in its proper place, Vincent invited her friends to four o'clock tea. She shined rosy apples to put in a bowl on a low table before the fire. She filled the cigarette boxes and brought out her finest tea service. Hattie, the housekeeper, made fancy sandwiches and laid logs in the fireplace. She felt so elegant pouring tea for her friends in her own house. The moments were all the more precious to her, for soon she was due to leave on a reading tour for Pittsburgh, Chicago, Iowa and other mid-western points. How she dreaded the thought of leaving Eugen behind and starting out alone.

Vincent traveled by train, sometimes giving two readings a day before women's clubs and literary audiences. The trains were dirty, the hotels uncomfortable and the journey tiring. She hated being away from Eugen. The only thing that sustained her was the fact that she had already paid off the bills in Camden and Rockland with money that she had earned, and the two thousand dollars which she would clear on this tour would help fill up the holes in her bank account.

To keep up her courage to continue the awful tour, Vincent told some people she met in Chicago that she and Eugen were going to Java and to China in March. With Eugen she felt she could do everything—even go around the earth. They had talked about it casually before she left. Now, her mind was made up—she wanted them to do it together. Even this tour would have been different if Eugen had been able to come along. She wouldn't have been so depressed about the hotels and baggage and dusty trains. It was the loneliness—even more than the discomfort—that was so wearying. Eugen was so gay and confident and had a way of making a game of everything.

After a month of this hard life, Vincent was still giving her readings with charm and verve, for she felt she owed it to the people who came to hear her to conceal her utter weariness and boredom. In Chicago she posed for an artist named Otto Schneider, who did a drawing of her, and in Milwaukee she met the mother and father of Dorothy Coleman, a Vassar friend who had died and to whom she had written the group of verses *Memorial to D. C.*

The tour finally did end. Though it was little more than a month, it had seemed much longer to Vincent. Eugen was waiting for her at the station in New York—his usual handsome, debonair self. Although Vincent had felt bedraggled and dusty throughout most of her journey, she had managed to rest and be shampooed and manicured at the end of it. All she wanted now was to be with Eugen in their snug brick house: to toast her toes before her own fire; to read her own books and to be with Eugen. She paused before the door to look again at the tiny house that was home. "It's good, good, good to be home," she told Eugen gravely, looking up at him with shining eyes. Eugen did not answer but swept her up in his arms and carried her over the threshold.

Vincent read and listened to music and occasionally went to the theater and opera. She could scarcely bear to leave her little house for too long a stretch and wanted so much to show it off to her family and friends. She went from one room to the other, wandering from the first floor to the third. Her elegant little home, with its arrangement of kitchen and dining room on the first floor and bedrooms at the top of the house, reminded her of the Millay home of her childhood in Camden by the brook, where she had spent so many happy hours with her piano and her poetry. This little house was warm and snug as the one in Camden never had been at this time of year. It was strange that her thoughts should be so much with that other little house, for living in an entire house in congested New York signified prosperity. In that other house, where there had never been money, there had been a richness of spirit and mind.

March came and went but still Vincent did not budge from Bedford Street. Eugen talked of going around the world and of the business he would attend to at the coffee plantations in Java and other far-flung places. Vincent sat in her deep, luxurious easy chair and studied the exotic pictures in the travel folders he brought her. Sometimes, it still seemed incredible to her that she—Vincent Millay of Camden, Maine—had won the Pulitzer Prize for poetry only a scant year before; that she was now married to this wonderfully kind and intelligent man, and could, whenever she wanted, take off for a trip around the world, traveling with every luxury she desired. She sometimes wondered if it seemed as incredible to other people as it did to her.

Spring came in April and now Vincent was eager to be off. She felt rested at last and well fed but hungry for new sights and sensations. Since their marriage, she and Eugen had not been anywhere together for an extended trip. He booked their passage to Japan on the S.S. *Taiyo Maru* and toward the end of the month they sailed eastward to meet the spring.

The S.S. *Taiyo Maru* docked at Hawaii. Vincent and Eugen spent eighteen perfect hours in Honolulu, swimming at Waikiki and sitting on the beach listening to the young boys strumming ukuleles. It was a beautiful semitropical country with a richly colored landscape and an abundance of exotic fruits and flowers. Eugen and Vincent were sorely tempted to spend more time there sunning themselves on the sand and eating bananas, pineapples and mangoes from the trees, but the wide world beckoned.

The day they left Hawaii, groups of native women came to the pier selling garlands of hibiscus flowers. Vincent brought one to throw overboard as an offering to the sea god so that someday they would be sure to return to this island paradise. The water was full of boys swimming about and diving for coins the passengers threw into the water. As the ship pulled away from the dock, the boys clambered up to the deck and then dived off to swim ashore. Vincent mailed a hibiscus flower from Hawaii to her sister Norma as the boat sailed toward Japan.

In Japan Vincent and Eugen visited Tokyo and Nikko. They were too late for the cherry blossoms in Tokyo but when they came to Nikko they found the double blossoms at their best and the single ones still in bloom. Never had Vincent seen anything comparable to the delicacy of the lacy pink tree branches against the blue sky, except perhaps a New England apple orchard in early spring. Determined now to leave cities behind them and travel off the beaten path, they took a walking trip through the mountain country with a coolie as a guide carrying their pack. They spent their nights at picturesque Japanese inns, sleeping on floor mats and eating meals of fish, rice and tea while sitting cross legged on the floor. When they came to the hot springs at Ikao, they found they could have as many hot baths as they wanted, for the water came from a bamboo pipe in the side of the mountain and flowed bubbling hot into a wooden tub all day. Their days in Japan were happy ones, and it was with both regret and anticipation that they sailed for China.

Their steamer docked at Shanghai and they made a two-day train trip to Peking, the old capital, where the last empress had lived in the walled Forbidden City. There they both became ill with the flu and had to stay in their hotel ten days, missing the major part of their sight-seeing.

When Vincent and Eugen recovered, they took a boat to Chefoo, a small village on the Yellow Sea. During the time they lived there they hired a junk and two Chinese sailors to man it for them. They sailed to a different island every day and Vincent later wrote a poem to the older of the boatmen. They swam and lay in the sun and gradually grew strong again. Vincent's special delight was building a fire on the shore to make coffee, for it was a real challenge in a Chinese seacoast village. There was no driftwood on the beaches since wood was scarce in China. The slim figure with the streaming red hair went up and down the beaches looking for wood to build her fire. Every day she scoured the sands for a nutshell, a few twigs and even bits of bottle corks with which to build a tiny fire, while they both grew brown and well.

Though it was hard to part from their Chinese junk and the man and boy who made up their crew and the good times on the beach, Vincent and Eugen made their way back to Shanghai to sail to Hong Kong on the S.S. *Anchies*. While the boat was loading cargo, Vincent and Eugen went ashore and found Hong Kong, a British possession, a city more Chinese than any in China proper. There was an aura of mystery and intrigue in the air that smelled of the East. It was the season of the monsoon and there were sudden downpours of rain, the like of which Vincent had never before seen. She hadn't known there was so much water in the world as managed to fall from the sky in a short hour or two.

They sailed on and between the monsoon storms there were beautiful bright rainbows in the spray of the ship as it plowed through the ocean. At night the phosphorous in the water made the edge of the waves a bright, electric green. It was so very beautiful that Vincent could scarcely believe it was she who was seeing these undreamed of beauties of the world. There was heat lightning, and standing at the railing watching the phosphorescent green of the waves, she said to her husband that the rainbows by day and the phosphorous by night was almost more beauty than she could bear.

He looked down with a tender smile and wondered aloud what would happen if she saw a rainbow at night.

Just then a rainbow, bright and perfect, hung low against the darkness of the sky in the wake of a flash of lightning and a few seconds later it disappeared as suddenly as it had come. Every fiber of Vincent's being responded to the strange beauty of the glowing rainbow of the night, and she recalled it whenever she turned back to the memories of the spell of the East and her long journey through it.

They sailed on to Batavia where it was hot and to Bandung in Java which was both beautiful and cool, and to all the exotic places that Vincent had dreamed about without ever expecting to see, and where Eugen had business connected with his coffee interests. By September they were in British India—Rangoon, Calcutta, Benares, Agra, Delhi, Jaipoor, Bombay—and from there they sailed directly to Marseilles. They planned to be in Paris by the middle of October and did not want to linger long in Europe. Vincent was anxious to be home by Thanksgiving and spend the holiday in her own dear little house with her own family. It was good to go all around the world, but it was good to be returning to the home hearth, too. Winter in New York was always the most interesting season.

Their little house on Bedford Street, snug and bright, enfolded them during the winter months. Their friends came to tea and they went to parties and the theater. Sometimes it seemed it would burst with their luggage and their souvenirs and their memories of gay times. Vincent went on reading tours—but not too far afield—Boston and Connecticut and once to Brunswick, Maine, to read at Bowdoin College. It was a great triumph for her to read her poems and to be listened to so respectfully in her own home state, with her husband at her side. This way, she enjoyed the readings as much as her audience.

It was spring and Vincent and Eugen had decided to move to the country. Eugen wanted to give up his coffee business and do some serious farming. Vincent thought perhaps she could work better without the distraction of city life, and she could just as well come into New York and stay at a hotel for a few days whenever she wanted to.

It was not without a twinge of regret that Vincent thought of leaving the little house on Bedford Street, but if they bought a country home there would be no rent to pay and space enough at last for the belongings they had managed to collect.

They began looking for a country house early in the spring and soon they had found a simple but beautiful farmhouse with seven hundred acres of land high in the mountain country at Austerlitz, New York, near the western border of Massachusetts. Eugen looked at the rolling pastures and Vincent looked at the beautiful mountains and the fields and meadows covered with the tall pink spires of the Steepletop plant.

"We'll call it Steepletop," Vincent cried, running waist high through a field of the weeds to the white clapboard house.

"Steepletop, it shall be," Eugen replied indulgently. His mind was busy with the crops he was planning to raise.

In the middle of June, Tufts College conferred the

honorary degree of Doctor of Letters on Edna St. Vincent
Millay and a week later the dignified new Dr. Millay was
busy overseeing the digging of holes and the laying of new
floors and the tearing down of old buildings at Steepletop,
her new home.

EIGHTEEN

Steepletop was renovated in one hectic summer. The simple white farmhouse was transformed into a gracious, modern home filled with books and fine paintings. There were two grand pianos at one end of the long living room. The rest of the room was furnished with comfortable easy chairs grouped around a fireplace. Wide windows looked out upon the trees where the birds nested.

With the masons and plumbers and carpenters swarming throughout the house and grounds, there was little rest. Eugen engaged twenty children to pick berries for the market. There were strawberries, huckleberries, currants, blueberries and blackberries and a continual hubbub. Vincent was forever discovering neglected patches of rhubarb and asparagus, brooks they didn't know existed on their property, and fields and meadows with dozens of fascinating flowers and weeds. When the summer was over, Steepletop had a varied farm of gardens and orchards and a cow. There was a garage with a guesthouse above it and a special little cabin high above in the woods where Vincent could be alone to work. And as the years progressed, Steepletop became known not as just another country estate with its own swimming pool and tennis courts and a jovial gentleman farmer indulging his inclination for haying and dairying, but almost as a sort of literary landmark.

Eugen had a genius for making friends and the house was filled with interesting people. Vincent's old friend

Arthur Ficke and his wife bought a place near by. Another friend, Esther Root, married Franklin P. Adams, who was known as F.P.A. on the "Information Please" radio program and wrote The Conning Tower, a famous literary column. They were all visitors at Steepletop, as well as Deems Taylor, Elinor Wylie, the Benéts, Edmund Wilson, Dorothy Thompson and scores of other people who had made their mark (or were about to) in the world of the arts.

Eugen hired servants to clean and cook. He did not want anything to distract Vincent from her work, for he believed her to be a true genius. He said that anyone could buy and sell coffee or run a farm, but that not many people could write an inspired poem. When Vincent was deep in the process of writing, she lost all sense of time. Eugen soon discovered that, though Vincent could bake wonderful bread and knew how to make delicious lobster stew, she might completely forget there were extra guests. So he himself undertook to order the meals and run the house with the servants. At the same time, he farmed actively and worked in the fields side by side with the men he hired. It was a good life for both of them. Arms linked, they would watch the sun setting behind the mountains on their beautiful acres, drinking in the beauty of the changing seasons and knowing peace in their own home.

Almost as soon as they had come to Steepletop, Vincent had begun having severe and steady headaches. Dark spots danced before her eyes and the world jumped around, giving her no peace. Nevertheless she worked on—taking the scraps of paper or notebooks in which she had written poems to the cabin in the woods or to the large studio over the garage with its windows in the treetops. She spread out her poems and studied them carefully. There was one about the Chinese boatman inspired by their trip around the world. She reread each poem carefully—crossing out one word and

substituting another—polishing and cutting and paring the
lines until she was completely satisfied. Often she kept a
poem for one or two years—sometimes ten—before she over-
came her doubts about publishing it.

Deems Taylor suggested that she write a libretto for an
opera. He would compose the opera, which had been commissioned by the Metropolitan Opera Company of New
York. Vincent was enthusiastic about the idea. It seemed big
and important—a real challenge to her ability. By the end of
November she had written one act. It was based on the story
of "Snow White and the Seven Dwarfs." By Christmas time,
Vincent decided that "Snow White and the Seven Dwarfs"
would not do. Charming as the theme was, it was too slight.
Discarding this, she began writing another drama which she
at first named "The Saxons." Throughout the winter, she
built blazing fires in her cabin in the woods and worked
hard at her manuscript. It was a long and complicated piece
of work, for she was determined to use only words known
in the English of that time. Her knowledge of early Anglo-
Saxon (which she had studied with such fascination at
Vassar) was an excellent basis for the searching and eliminat-
ing of the anachronisms that sometimes crept in. Even so,
her head was always in the big dictionary. She worked at the
manuscript steadily through the winter and most of the summer. Scene by scene, she sent the opera to Deems Taylor,
revised it here and there, and he set it to music. Her early
music lessons were a help. Sometimes it seemed to Vincent
that everything she was and everything she knew were
being used to create the opera.

In the autumn the singers were already rehearsing the first
act. Vincent was kept busy correcting the proof on *The
King's Henchman,* as the opera was finally called. It was so
exciting that Vincent decided she must go somewhere; she
couldn't just sit still. Eugen wanted a change, too, so they

packed their bags and went to visit Arthur and Gladys Ficke in Santa Fe, New Mexico. They returned to Steepletop in midwinter to be near New York in time for the opening night of *The King's Henchman*.

Life was overflowing with good things for the other Millays, too. Norma was singing the role of Serpetta in Harrison Dowd's poetic adaptation of the German libretto of Mozart's opera *La Finta Giardiniera* which was produced by The Intimate Opera Company at the Mayfair Theater in New York. Kathleen and her husband Howard were in New York. Vincent sent for her mother, for how could there be this world première at the Metropolitan Opera House without Mother Millay?

Vincent looked at herself in the mirror and wondered if her hair had perhaps turned a darker shade of red—perhaps almost brown. Her mirror reflected an unlined, elfin face with a marked look of innocence. Her hair was neatly bobbed and her body small and slim. Her quick, birdlike movements betokened more a girl in her teens than a woman of thirty-four. Vincent walked away from the mirror and decided she would have the dress from Paris after all. She was sure it would suit her and it was her heart's desire.

The evening of February 17 came at last. Vincent sat safely beside Eugen for one last moment in the darkness of the car before they drew up to the brilliantly lighted entrance of the Metropolitan Opera House. Sleek, black limousines all about them were disgorging beautifully gowned women escorted by men in formal evening dress. The wealthy and the celebrated, the cream of society and the intelligentsia, opera lovers from all walks of life and the music critics of all the important papers were milling about in anticipatory excitement. Everybody had turned out for the world première of *The King's Henchman*.

Vincent swept up the stairs to her box in her shimmering

red velvet evening gown—the tiny train trailing out behind her like a fishtail. She had always wanted a bright red dress, but because of the color of her hair she thought she couldn't have it. Now she had it and she could tell it was right from the hushed whispers of the people who stood aside to clear a path for her and nudged one another saying, "There goes Edna St. Vincent Millay!" How happy she was that she had had the courage to buy it after all. It was another dream come true.

Deems and his wife made room for Vincent and Eugen in their box. They all bent over the programs which were more than familiar to them and looked at each other fearfully. For a few awful moments they wondered why they had ever ventured into such a fearful situation. It was almost bound to be a failure, for there was that line that needed polishing and that bar of music that should have been changed. Somewhere out there in the vast audience sat Mother Millay and Kathleen and Howard and Norma and Charles. If only she had been circumspect enough not to invite her family, Vincent thought dolefully; then they, at least, would be spared witnessing her failure. She borrowed Eugen's opera glasses to scan the audience, searching for them. The most awful thing about an opera was that it was a public spectacle. If a book failed, it was easy to hide at home. Here she had to sit in public view, and should the music be badly played or a singer sing a flat note or muddle a line, she would have to suffer through it. She wondered as she regarded Deems if the audience ever felt impelled to single out the composer and the librettist as well as the performers when an opera displeased them.

The orchestra struck up the first notes of the overture. Vincent had been playing the score on the piano for months and knew almost every note. How pure and true they were playing tonight. She shivered with pleasure. Her fears were

all gone. She could hardly wait for the great golden curtain
to rise on the first scene. Were they really *her* words they
were singing? Everything seemed so right on the stage. One
impressive scene succeeded another. The costumes and the
scenery were lovelier than she had imagined. The full orchestra, playing the music, immeasurably enriched the words
and story. As Vincent sat there following every note and
every word and gesture, it was a thing apart. She enjoyed
and appreciated each word anew—exactly as if she hadn't
written it—and the music was as fresh to her ears as if she
had never heard a note of it.

The curtain slowly fell on the last majestic strains of the
first act. The houselights were turned on amid deafening
applause. *The King's Henchman* was a first-night success.
Vincent knew it instinctively and confirmed it by looking
over at Deems, who no longer looked tense and on edge. She
flew from the box in search of her mother. People she knew
and people she didn't know stopped to congratulate her.
At last she spied her mother's happy face.

"I couldn't be prouder of you, Sefe," Mother Millay said.

"Oh, Mother! Isn't it wonderful! Wonderful!" Vincent
exclaimed quite immodestly, for by now her part in the opera
seemed infinitesimal. "It's all so perfect I don't know how
I'm going to bear it."

Vincent and Deems followed each succeeding scene more
critically now. They had both been so overwhelmed at first
that they couldn't think, but now they made notes on the
margins of the score to help improve future performances.

When the curtain rang down on the last act and the
singers bowed for the last time to the applause of the audience, there were cries of "Bravo! Bravo!" They called loudly
for the composer and librettist, and the blinding spotlight
picked out Deems Taylor and Edna St. Vincent Millay in
their box in the golden horseshoe. Deems stood up to bow

and Vincent, tiny and slight in her bright red dress beside him, waved a small white hand in acknowledgment. The thunder of clapping hands deafened her and the sound seemed to roll over her like a wave. It was like a dream. In a fraction of a second, Vincent remembered that it had been a dream. She was transported back to her childhood when she dreamed of being a concert pianist, receiving applause and adulation on the stage in a green brocade gown. She hadn't even dared to *dream* of a red dress then. This was better than her dream, for a piano concert is soon over. The opera would live on if it were good enough to endure. The libretto would be printed as a dramatic poem in book form. Her moment in the spotlight and the applause were sweet. Vincent hadn't felt so triumphant since her graduation from high school when she had read her own poem in the Camden Opera House.

There was a gay party afterward, for no one could think of going to sleep on an opening night until the morning papers came out with the critics' reviews. In the midst of the champagne toasts and gaieties, the papers were brought in. *The King's Henchman* was hailed as an event in American opera. It was received with excitement and good will. The party became gayer—there was praise for the composer, for the music and richness of the orchestration and to the librettist for the musical words of the book. *The King's Henchman* was hailed as the first really good American opera sung by performers who knew English. The singers—especially Lawrence Tibbett who sang the role of the king— came in for their share of praise. Even the stage settings were acclaimed as unusually good. It seemed to Vincent that all her dreams and her longings and many-faceted talents had coalesced into that one evening—her love of music and the stage and her early attempts to succeed in them, her poetry, the first and last of her loves, and her chosen vocation and her need for the assurance of success. She was so glad that it had happened at such a right time. Eugen was proud of her and Mother Millay's faith in her was vindicated. The evening was beyond her wildest dreams from beginning to end.

On the way home Vincent tried to voice some of her thoughts to Eugen. "You know, Eugen, everything I ever dreamed of as a child came true for me tonight," she began thoughtfully. "Do you suppose that anything else lies before me?"

"It's time to put away childish dreams," Eugen replied gently. "The whole world of ideas is before you—serious ideas."

"That's true, dear." Vincent pounced upon the thought with the keen swiftness of her mind. "It's the poet's mission in life to blazon a path of ideas—to see about things like peace and justice. I guess there are still other worlds for me to conquer."

Vincent's work did become more serious. The quick, personal aspect of her poetry still remained but to it was added the desire to fight for a cause. Her sense of social consciousness came to the fore more and more often. When Elinor Wylie was barred from the League of American Penwomen, Vincent wrote the organization an indignant letter, though she herself had been invited as guest of honor at their principal function in Washington. She was always a willing fighter in the interests of poetry and poets, quick and generous with her time and efforts. Now more than ever she extended her range.

Vincent's sense of justice was outraged by the Sacco-Vanzetti case. In 1920 two Italian anarchists named Sacco and Vanzetti were accused of killing a shoe factory paymaster and his guard in South Braintree, Massachusetts. Though there were serious doubts concerning their guilt, the two men were sentenced to death in 1927. Vincent—together with many other intellectuals—fought the death penalty and did everything in her power to commute the sentence. Along with many others, she felt that they were being put to death as much for the ideas they upheld as for a crime.

The day before the execution, Vincent called on Governor Fuller of Massachusetts to plead with him for clemency for the condemned men. She called the Governor's attention to the fact that the death penalty had been outlawed in her own state of Maine following the hanging of an innocent man for a crime he did not commit. After the interview, she wrote the Governor an impassioned letter, pleading with him to change his mind. Vincent's story was attacked on grounds of veracity, and her participation in the case became a matter of public controversy.

She did not content herself with merely writing letters and articles and important interviews with the Governor. She took part in a protest demonstration in front of the State Capitol in Boston, carrying a placard which read, "If these men are executed Justice is dead in Massachusetts." As she walked about briskly on the narrow, hilly street, steadying her banner, she could look over at John Dos Passos, Jack Lawson and the other writers who were participating in the demonstration. The frivolities of life seemed far away. Nothing was as important as stirring up public opinion and making the complaisant citizens of Massachusetts realize that a great injustice was being inflicted upon innocent men by their state government. As the small, brave band of liberal intellectuals pressed on in their march for justice, a group of policemen appeared and suddenly surrounded them and maneuvered them aside. They were formally arrested for "sauntering and loitering," loaded into a police car and driven off to jail where they were placed in cells. They sang and recited poetry to one another to keep up their spirits during the long, weary hours before bail for their release could be arranged. Despite all that Vincent and the many others who had taken up the cause could do, Sacco and Vanzetti were put to death.

The aftermath of the Sacco-Vanzetti case was as strenuously controversial as it was at the time of the trial. Vincent was busy answering the attacks on some of her statements and writings. In October she and the five others who had been arrested for their street demonstration in Boston were brought back again for their trial. They planned to plead "not guilty" and refuse to pay any fine, going to jail if necessary to keep public opinion alive on the subject. After several delays, they were finally acquitted in December.

In the meantime, Vincent was writing on the subject in every conceivable form. Her article for *Outlook* magazine called "Fear" was an inspired and inspiring call for justice. Although she had thrown all her energies and most of her waking hours into fighting for an ideal, her own harvest was rich. There was a group of poems inspired by the Sacco-Vanzetti case—"The Anguish," "Justice Denied in Massachusetts," "Hangman's Oak," "Wine from These Grapes," "To Those Without Pity"—which showed a new vein in Vincent's talent, a deep, impassioned feeling for an impersonal cause. The floodgates of her writing seemed to be released. She worked steadily and well.

She wanted to have enough poems to bring out a new book. Abby Evans, her old friend from Camden, with whom she used to climb Mount Megunticook and compare poems, was having a book of poetry published. Strangely enough, now it was Vincent who led the way, for the publishers asked her to make the selection and write a short preface for the book.

Soon Vincent's next book *The Buck in the Snow* appeared. Coming as it did after the Pulitzer prize-winning volume and containing her astoundingly different poems of social protest, *The Buck in the Snow* attracted wide attention but received mixed reviews. Max Eastman, who reviewed it for the *Nation*, liked it very much and chided some of the other reviewers for following like sheep the bellwether fashion to be "disappointed" in it. The British press also praised it highly, and the public had reason now to expect and respect many more aspects in the poetry of Edna St. Vincent Millay.

NINETEEN

Though her interests had taken a new and serious direction, Vincent still had time for gaiety. There were trips abroad—to Paris or England—and when the winter snows palled on them, Vincent and Eugen packed up and went to get warm in the Florida sun.

There were beginning to be more neighbors near Steepletop. Arthur Ficke, Vincent's dear old friend, had built a house not far away and called it "Hardhack," which was another name for the steepletop weed. By the summer of 1930, their friends the Branns and the LaBranches had new houses near by. Vincent decided to give a large party to welcome them. One week end in July, they all filled their homes with guests. When the gigantic four-way house party was assembled, there were between fifty or sixty people for the week end. Vincent engaged the Jitney Players, a theatrical touring company, to give a performance during the evening. During the day she planned to have a fair to entertain her guests.

The day before the party she and Eugen, John Pinney and everyone else they could muster were busy hammering and sawing and building booths for the fair grounds. The gaily striped awnings, the areas set aside for games, the stands for food and punch scattered about Steepletop began to take on the aspect of a miniature county fair on a velvety green lawn.

People began coming to the fair the next day. There were

poets and musicians, artists and writers, actors and plain, ordinary people. Deems Taylor manned the hot dog stand. He made himself a cocked hat that he wore jauntily down on his forehead, and wielded his large fork dextrously as he put broiled frankfurters into split rolls and courteously asked, "Mustard? Piccalilli? Both or one?" Arthur Ficke mixed and served drinks near the swimming pool in the shade of the cedar hedge. There were games of chance and prizes— silly prizes that were fun. The party went on and on like some of the Paris parties during Vincent's first trip abroad. Nobody slept and nobody ate regular meals—just hot dogs and popcorn and candied apples. The punch bowl was always full. The Jitney Players found the perfect spot to stage their play in the evening—a long slope reaching up toward the mountains. They set up their props, the audience sat down in the grass and the play began. It was amusing and light and well presented.

Vincent and Eugen wandered among the guests—as happy as two birds on the wing. She felt like a child at play and remembered the happy times of her childhood when she had gone to the fair.

"Doesn't this remind you of Union Fair?" Vincent asked Norma in passing. "Do you remember when we used to go to Union Fair and all the fun we had there?" She didn't wait for a reply, but immediately started telling Eugen about it and to ask whether there were any fairs in Holland with all the amusements for children. The fair continued for several days until the hosts, the guests, the food and drink were all exhausted. Still singing and dancing, they bade each other a merry farewell and went home with their happy memories, leaving Steepletop to return to peaceful quiet.

A month later Vincent went to Boston to speak at the Memorial Meeting for Sacco and Vanzetti on the third anniversary of their execution. She and Eugen stayed at a historic house in Cambridge which had been Washington's headquarters for almost a year during the Revolution. Longfellow had lived there for a time with his family and Vincent and Eugen ate lunch with Longfellow's grandson. In speaking out for liberty and justice and courage from the pulpit of the Old South Church, Vincent was continuing the spirit of freedom from tyranny that had been part of her country's tradition since its inception. She was like a flame as she made her impassioned speech, asking the people to put aside fear and rally to be free. Most impressive of all was her reading of the five poems inspired by the case.

Then Vincent went to see Mother Millay to tell her of the honor that had been paid her as she used to bring her flowers as a child. For it was indeed remarkable that the child from Camden grew up to be the woman who addressed the meeting in Boston. No one was more aware of it than Vincent herself. The bond between Vincent and her mother had deepened and never wavered as the years passed and Vincent went from pinnacle to pinnacle of success and honor.

The following February, when the news came that Mother Millay had died, Vincent could scarcely believe that they were talking to *her* about *her* mother. She became numb all over and couldn't even cry. It was Eugen who had to make all the practical arrangements. Almost before she knew it, he had packed their bags and whisked her off to Camden. As soon as Vincent saw her mother, quiet and peaceful and so still, the awful finality of death was brought home to her. She would have given anything to have her mother back and alive—all her fame, all her triumphs which now seemed so unimportant, all her wealth. Vincent and Norma and Kathleen took Mother Millay away to be buried at Steepletop. How Vincent hated to see her mother lowered into the hard, unyielding ground in the dead of winter. She had always so hated the cold.

For months the memory of her last glimpse of her mother haunted Vincent. Almost involuntarily, she found her thoughts turning to her time and again, and it was difficult to realize that she wasn't there any more. How many times she would have liked to tell her something or write to her or ask her advice only to realize with a start that never again could she do so. It was like coming out of anesthesia. Facing reality was the hardest part of all. Her mother's death made Vincent a sadder and wiser person. It made her appreciate all the more the many things that Eugen had done for her, and she resolved to carry on her duties more conscientiously. They dismissed their servants and Vincent spent half the day in cleaning and in household chores and the rest out of doors. Eugen worked the farm and the gardens. In time they resumed their good life of travel abroad for interest and stimulation, to Florida to bask in the sun, or sometimes to the French Riviera, and entertaining their many friends both in New York and at Steepletop.

Vincent threw herself into her work. She was not only writing poetry. She was pioneering for poetry in a new direction. In December of 1932, she began broadcasting over the radio on a nation-wide hookup. On eight Sunday evenings she read her own poems. She was terrified of the little black microphone, and prayed people would not snap off their radios when they heard her voice. It was a great responsibility for one small, frail, red-haired woman to carry on her shoulders, for it was the first time in the history of radio broadcasting that the public was presumed to be interested enough in literature to listen to a poet on the same par with a singer or an actress. Vincent need not have worried. Her voice—deep and thrilling and unimaginably expressive—reached into the hearts of millions of people. When her fan mail started pouring in and the studio tabulated it for her, Vincent was as excited as a little girl. The readings were tremendously successful.

Vincent had scarcely recovered from the broadcasts—which had almost completely exhausted her—and helped Eugen put the gardens at Steepletop into shape, when it was time for her to go to New York and Wisconsin to become a Doctor of Literature twice. That June at their graduation exercises both Russell Sage College and the University of Wisconsin conferred honorary degrees upon her.

For some time now, both Eugen and Vincent had been missing the sea. Steepletop was beautiful—high and rimmed around by the majesty of mountains. But they had both grown up in coastal regions. Vincent, especially, sometimes felt closed in at Steepletop and longed for the endless horizon of the ocean of her native Maine. So early in the summer they bought Ragged Island, one of the least accessible of the islands in lower Casco Bay. It was a wild, exciting place with dark spruce trees crowding to the edge of its steep cliffs. Only one house stood on the island. There Vincent and Eugen intended to spend August in peace and quiet, living roughly, close to the elements of sun and wind and rain, surrounded by the sea.

Unfortunately, Vincent became ill with the flu during the summer and had to stay in bed for days at a time. They were not able to go to Ragged Island the summer they bought it, but almost every summer after that, they spent many happy months there, swimming and fishing, cooking out of doors and eating their fill of the lobsters that Eugen hauled from his traps.

Her lingering weakness did not deter Vincent from writing poetry. She worked day and night at it, writing new poems and revamping the old ones. Within a year she had collected enough of her own poetry for a new volume. *Wine from These Grapes* was published on November 1, 1934.

The period from 1933 to 1938 marked some of the most productive and varied years of Vincent's literary career. After publishing *Wine from These Grapes* she began translating with George Dillon, a poet and friend, some of the poetry from the French of Baudelaire. After this volume was published as *Flowers of Evil* on April 2, 1936 (because Vincent refused to be published on April Fools' Day) she began working on a long dramatic work called *Conversation at Midnight*. It was a poetic discussion of the philosophy of life of men of different beliefs and stations. Even before the translations had gone to press, Vincent was hard at work on this original play in verse dealing with the ideas and philosophies of men. In May of 1936, she and Eugen went to Sanibel Island, a lovely, unspoiled spot off the coast of Florida. They arrived at their hotel about an hour before sunset. So eager was she to go to the beach to gather sea shells she didn't even go up to see their room. When Vincent looked back from the beach a few minutes later, the hotel was in flames. All of her luggage and the partly completed manuscript of *Conversation at Midnight* were burned.

Vincent mourned the loss of her cherished little seventeenth century copy of *Catullus, Propertius and Tibullus*, from which she used to read a few passages of Latin poetry every night, more than all her clothes and luggage and the valuable emerald ring that were burned in the fire.

Back at Steepletop she began the painful task of reconstructing her burnt manuscript. The passages that had been finished and were ready for publication she could recall from memory. By saying them over and over aloud, she was able to rewrite them exactly as they had stood. The sections that were unfinished were still vague in her mind. Even after the play was completed and published the following summer she was still not sure whether some of the best of her poetry had not been burned in the fire.

Although Vincent and Eugen had only a vague inkling of it while it was happening, this was a summer of misfortune. One night while riding in their station wagon they took a sharp turn, the door flew open and Vincent was thrown out. It was a strange and horrible sensation to be hurled out so forcefully into the pitch-black night. She rolled over and over down a rocky gully, bumping over the stones until she managed to catch hold of some bushes. When Eugen ran to find her she was sobbing with fright. Though she had a big bump on her head and was scratched and bruised all over, she tried to make light of it when Eugen finally got her to the house and examined her for broken bones. Her right arm was wrenched and she could not use it for a long time. But the real extent of her injury and its seriousness did not manifest itself until about four years later.

During June of 1937 Vincent received the honorary degree of Doctor of Human Letters from New York University, and in July *Conversation at Midnight* was published. Neither event was an unmitigated joy for Vincent. Because she was barred from a dinner given for all the other recipients of honorary degrees conferred by New York University that year on account of her sex, she felt impelled to write a letter to the chancellor protesting against the discrimination. She would have refused the degree if she could have done it privately, without causing talk. And there were still nagging doubts in her mind that certain magical phrases from *Conversation at Midnight* had not been lost forever in the fire.

Now she felt more impelled than ever to make her next book of poetry perfect. Within two years *Huntsman, What Quarry?* was off the press. It was the first book that Vincent had ever gotten to the printer on time. She wondered whether it was a bad omen. She could not know then that it was, in a sense, the last book she herself would publish of what she considered her "real" poetry.

The injury Vincent had sustained four years before in her fall from the station wagon now became chronic. From an occasional twinge in her back and the intermittent loss of the use of her right arm due to what she thought was bursitis under her shoulder blade, the symptoms began to make themselves felt so that she was in constant pain. Ten or twelve doctors finally diagnosed it as an injury to certain nerves in her back, and within the next year she had three operations which were supposed to effect a cure. She was very weak, but she hoped she would in time grow stronger.

In the meantime the war in Europe had already broken out. The Nazi invasion of Czechoslovakia particularly affected Vincent, for she had known and loved the country during her early years abroad. She turned her thoughts and her pen to the aid of the oppressed long before her country joined the war and long before the majority of her countrymen recognized the danger.

She wrote a series of poems that she thought of as "impassioned propaganda" and published them in 1940 long before she ordinarily would have, had they been personal poems. *Make Bright the Arrows* was its title. She hoped that the subtitle "1940 Notebook" would explain to the public and the critics that though some of it was not up to her usual standard, she wanted them read more as propaganda than as poetry. She hoped that the good poems (which happened to be propaganda, too) would overcome the effect of some of the not wholly finished work. Much of it had been done during the long months she had had to spend in the hospitals, and that, too, had not helped improve its quality.

Her new book had some reviews favorable beyond her expectations, but some of her old friends with grown sons accused her of attempting to incite her country to war. She felt however, that she had to do something to stop the terrible thing that was happening to the free countries of Europe. She was willing to sacrifice even her reputation as a poet to the cause in which she believed.

In constant pain for almost two years, Vincent now hoped to get better under the care of a new doctor. Eugen had lost the greater part of his fortune due to the war, and the constant bills for doctors and hospitals, X Rays and medicines began to drain their financial resources. The Boissevains were never again to know the easy affluence of wealth. In spite of her recurrent illness, Vincent now felt it was up to her to recoup the family fortunes.

In April and August she made some recordings of her poems for RCA Victor. She was well paid and hoped some of them would be good propaganda for the call to freedom. The pain she now suffered was so excruciating that Eugen— gray with anxiety and desperate—was even quicker than the doctor to give her the prescribed dose of morphine.

TWENTY

When the United States entered the war actively in December, 1941, Vincent was determined to do everything she could to help, and to vindicate her reputation. From her point of view, the actual outbreak of the war at Pearl Harbor was simply a visible sign of something that had been in existence for some time. That was why she was ready with four poems on the war. She knew now that she had made a mistake in publishing *Make Bright the Arrows*. The reviewers had been very critical of her poems and she had been attacked on all sides. She had sacrificed her reputation, but it had done no good. The Americans who read the poems did not understand why she had written these verses, nor were they concerned with her reason for so hurriedly publishing them. She hoped to make the new works both good poetry and effective propaganda. The first of the four poems appeared in the magazine section of the New York *Sunday Times* three weeks after the United States entered the war.

The war came closer to Vincent than to most people. Before the month was over, her cousin Lieutenant Colonel George Ricker was reported missing over southern California in an Air Force plane. Eugen's family in Holland were not able to communicate with him, and they feared the worst.

Vincent and Eugen changed their way of life radically. Although Steepletop was a working farm and they were entitled to an allotment of gasoline on that basis, they gave up automobiles for the duration. They drove to and from Austerlitz to pick up their mail and groceries in a horse and buggy. In spite of their worries and fears, they made light of their sacrifices and turned them into something gay and whimsical. Who would not enjoy setting out for town on a dewy spring morning down the flower-strewn road in an open surrey? In winter Eugen negotiated the six miles on snowshoes. Although that was arduous, it did not quench his spirit. These small inconveniences were not important in the face of what his relatives were enduring in Holland.

The electric generator used forty gallons of gasoline a day, so they dispensed with electric lights. Vincent thought the dimness restful and a little romantic. It recalled her childhood before the era of bright lighting. She found herself able to read and write just as well by candlelight. It was in the soft light of the candles that she wrote an urgent essay pointing out that the pursuit of happiness did not necessarily mean chasing a "good time." She begged her fellow countrymen to make the sacrifices necessary to win the war.

Vincent threw herself into war work. She was a member of the Writers' War Board, the Red Cross and played a leading part in the wartime New York *Times* Conference of Women. At the same time, she wanted to continue writing her own poetry. She had felt guilty when the Poetry Society of America presented her with their gold medal at the annual dinner in January of 1943. She had been doing so many other things that sometimes she felt like anything but a poet. She resolved to continue her war work but to make time and get enough money to devote herself to her own poetry.

During the war Vincent's pleasures remained simple—watching the birds nest and hatch and following them to maturity, gardening more than ever for the food it yielded as well as the pleasure, picking flowers and seeing now a somewhat limited group of old friends.

When the war ended, this simpler pattern of life continued. Their nearest neighbor Arthur Davison Ficke, whom Vincent loved dearly, was slowly dying of a fatal disease. This had a sobering effect upon her. She did not want to see too many people—in particular new people. There was no desire—and now no money—to resume the lavish life of large parties, travel and winters on the French Riviera and in Florida.

Arthur died on November 30, 1945. He was buried at Hardhack, his home in neighboring Hillsdale. At his grave Vincent read the sonnet she had written to him, "And you as well must die, beloved dust," and passages from one of his favorite poems, Milton's "Lycidas."

Returning from the funeral with Eugen, Vincent felt like a lost child. Arthur had represented—perhaps more than anyone else except Norma—her transition from the eager child in Camden, Maine, to the foremost poetess of her generation. He had known her and her work—and he knew her mind so intimately—longer even than Eugen. Being a poet himself, he had been her hope and comfort and encouragement. He had understood her in all her varied moods. "I don't know how we're going to get on without him," Vincent sobbed, breaking into tears at last. "How are we ever going to get used to his not being here?"

Arthur's death gave rise to some sobering thoughts. Vincent soon wrote to Harper and Brothers, her publishers, ordering them never to alter one word of her published poetry after her death. She told them that the faults as well as the virtues of her poems were her own, and she wanted no one meddling with them when she was dead. She did not include hastily written and what she called "hotheaded" pieces as were some of the passages in *Make Bright the Arrows* and *The Murder of Lidice,* which she regarded as primarily war propaganda.

Just as Vincent had feared and anticipated, her "bad"

poetry had marred her reputation as a serious poet. No matter how much she explained, she still could not make everyone understand that her propaganda was supposed to be in an entirely different category from her serious work. There were murmurs and rumors, reviews and surveys explaining that Edna St. Vincent Millay's poetic muse had run dry. She had made the extreme sacrifice for patriotism—the reputation and career she had so carefully built by hard work and tedious hours as well as talent and inspiration for some twenty-five years. Now she had to begin again—almost at the beginning.

The simple life that Vincent and Eugen led—Steepletop was their home and they summered at Ragged Island—was good for the writing of poetry. As in her childhood, all but the essentials of life were dispensed with. Vincent began experimenting with new, freer forms of poetry. As long as she was able to write and express herself, she was happy. She spent many hours watching birds and memorizing the poetry of other poets whom she admired—from the Latin poet Catullus to contemporary Gerard Hopkins.

Vincent worked with a will at her new poetry. She wanted to bring out a book of good poetry. Her publishers were anxious for a book of hers to be printed—or even reprinted. Vincent would not be deflected. Because of the propaganda poetry she had written during the war, she was even more careful and critical than before of her work. She wrote very slowly, and she sometimes worked from morning till night—forgetting all else. Communication with the outside world became less important both to Eugen and Vincent. During the summer on Ragged Island they were cut off entirely from everybody except the chosen few they allowed to visit them. At Steepletop they eventually even went so far as to have the telephone disconnected because the world intruded on them more than they wished.

It was in this atmosphere of seclusion that Eugen suddenly

discovered that he was critically ill and needed a serious operation. There had been no symptoms, he had seemed healthy and well and had experienced no pain. He entered Deaconess Hospital in Boston for the operation. On August 30, 1949, he died. His death was attributed to shock following the operation.

Vincent could not long withstand Eugen's death. With him gone, a great part of her died, too. Her constant companion for twenty-six years, the most devoted of husbands, the gayest of men, the most understanding of human creatures, he was truly irreplaceable. Vincent became ill and was in a New York hospital again for months.

When she had recovered sufficiently to leave, she decided to return alone to Steepletop against the advice of doctors, nurses, editors and friends.

It took all of Vincent's courage to go back to the house where she had been so happy with Eugen. Once inside and settled again, it was not nearly as hard as she imagined it would be. It was almost a comfort to be again where he had lived—to be reminded of their happiness—to touch the things he had used—reread the books they had read together.

The holidays were the hardest times for her. For the first time in her life, she spent Thanksgiving Day alone. This holiday had always been so joyful and meaningful for her, but she could not celebrate it this year. She pretended it was just another day, for she did not want to distress anybody else with her grief. It was the same with all the other happy holidays that year.

Vincent now lived only because she hadn't died. She nursed herself back to health and tried to attend to all the practical matters of paying taxes and writing checks. She wanted to be brave for Eugen's sake, for she knew he would not like her to shirk her responsibilities.

Somehow, Vincent got through the spring, though when

she found the first dandelion of the season she could not ignore it. Her face crumpled and she began to cry. Her sense of loss was immense.

When summer came she was inured to the flowers and the sky and the grass. She could bear them once again. *The Saturday Evening Post* commissioned her to write a Thanksgiving poem. Although it was a minor event in her career, it showed her that she had not been entirely forgotten in the world of literature. She set about writing the poem with as much zeal as if it were to be an important milestone in her work. It was so wonderful to be writing again that nothing mattered. It helped her to get through August—which was a bad period for her—the first anniversary of Eugen's death. It was a great satisfaction for her when she had made the poem as faultless as she knew how, neatly retyped it and mailed it to the magazine.

Autumn came to Steepletop in its full glory. Vincent kept herself busy bedding down her garden for the winter, for she did not want a single bush or flower to die because it had not been properly wrapped and protected. Rolfe Humphries, whose poetry she admired, asked her to write an opinion of his latest work, a translation of the *Aeneid*. Vincent settled herself comfortably on the floor to work on the proofs, spreading the long sheaves of galley paper all about her. She read steadily. It was a good time, for she could think so well and clearly alone in the stillness of the night. She started for bed almost at dawn. As she reached the curve of the staircase, she felt a sudden sharp pain. Steadying herself, she sat down on the stairs. Before she could cry out, her life was over.

This was the life of Edna St. Vincent Millay. Even in death, it cast "a lovely light."

The poems which she had been writing for the last ten years were published after her death. *Mine the Harvest* contained some of her finest and most inspired poetry.

The Complete Works of Edna St. Vincent Millay

POEMS

Renascence and Other Poems. New York: M. Kennerley, 1917; also, New York: Harper & Bros., 1928.

Second April. New York: M. Kennerley, 1921; also, New York: Harper & Bros., 1921.

A Few Figs from Thistles. New York: F. Shay, 1921; also, New York and London: Harper & Bros., 1922.

The Harp Weaver and Other Poems. New York and London: Harper & Bros., 1923.

The Buck in the Snow and Other Poems. New York and London: Harper & Bros., 1928.

Poems Selected for Young People. New York and London: Harper & Bros., 1929.

Fatal Interview. New York and London: Harper & Bros., 1931.

Wine from These Grapes. New York and London: Harper & Bros., 1934.

Huntsman, What Quarry? New York and London: Harper & Bros., 1939.

Collected Lyrics of Edna St. Vincent Millay. New York: Harper & Bros., 1939.

Collected Sonnets of Edna St. Vincent Millay. New York and London: Harper & Bros., 1941.

Mine the Harvest. New York: Harper & Bros., 1954.

Collected Poems. New York: Harper & Bros., 1956.

WORLD WAR II POETRY

Make Bright the Arrows; 1940 Notebook. New York and London: Harper & Bros., 1940.

There Are No Islands, Any More; lines written in passion and deep concern for England, France and my own country. New York and London: Harper & Bros., 1940.

The Murder of Lidice. New York and London: Harper & Bros., 1942.

Poem and Prayer for an Invading Army. New York: National Broadcasting Co., 1944. (Written for NBC and read by Ronald Colman, June 6, 1944 over the NBC network.)

PLAYS

The Wall of Dominoes. Vassar Miscellany Monthly, May 1917.

Aria da Capo; a play in one act. New York: Harper & Bros., 1920.

The Lamp and the Bell; a drama in five acts. New York and London: Harper & Bros., 1921.

Two Slatterns and a King; a moral interlude. Cincinnati: Stewart Kidd Co., 1921.

Three Plays: Two Slatterns and a King, Aria da Capo, The Lamp and the Bell. New York and London: Harper & Bros., 1926.

The King's Henchman; a play in three acts. New York and London: Harper & Bros., 1927. This poem, slightly abridged, was the libretto for the opera: *The King's Henchman;* lyric drama in three acts. Book by Edna St. Vincent Millay, Music by Deems Taylor. New York: F. Rullman, Inc., 1927.

The Princess Marries the Page, a play in one act. New York and London: Harper & Bros., 1932.

Conversation at Midnight. New York and London: Harper & Bros., 1937.

OTHER PUBLISHED WORKS

Distressing Dialogues by Nancy Boyd (pseudonym). New York: Harper Bros., 1924.

Fear. New York: *The Outlook,* 1927.

Flowers of Evil by Charles Pierre Baudelaire. Translated from the French by George Dillon and Edna St. Vincent Millay. New York and London: Harper & Bros., 1936.

Invocation to the Muses. New York and London: Harper & Bros., 1941. (Read at the public ceremonial of the National Institute of Arts and Letters at Carnegie Hall, New York, January 18, 1941.)

Adventure in Radio; with radio scripts by Edna St. Vincent Millay, Arch Obler, Archibald MacLeish and others; edited by Margaret Cuthbert Ross. New York: Howell, Soskin, Inc., 1945.

Letters of Edna St. Vincent Millay; edited by Allan Ross Macdougall. New York: Harper & Bros., 1952.

Selected Bibliography about
Edna St. Vincent Millay

Atkins, Elizabeth. *Edna St. Vincent Millay and Her Times*. Chicago: The University of Chicago Press, 1936.

Benet, William Rose. "Round About Parnassus," *Saturday Review of Literature*, November 10, 1934.

Bogan, Louise. "Conversion into Self," *Poetry*, February 1935.

Brenner, Rica. *Ten Modern Poets*. New York: Harcourt, Brace and Co., 1930.

Burton, Katherine. "Edna Millay," *Commonweal*, March 11, 1938.

Bynner, Witter. "Edna St. Vincent Millay," *New Republic*, December 10, 1924.

DuBois, Arthur E. "Edna St. Vincent Millay," *Sewanee Review*, 1935.

Ferguson, C. W. "Miss Millay Goes Over the Top," *Bookman*, March, 1927.

Flanner, Hildegarde. "Two Poets: Jeffers and Millay," *New Republic*, January 27, 1937.

Humphries, Rolfe. "Miss Millay As Artist," *Nation*, December 20, 1941.
                   "Edna St. Vincent Millay, 1892-1950," *Nation*, December 30, 1950.

Mearns, Hughes (ed.). *Edna St. Vincent Millay*, New York: Simon & Schuster, 1927.

Monroe, Harriet. "Edna St. Vincent Millay," *Poetry*, August, 1924.
                   "Advance or Retreat?", *Poetry*, July, 1931.

Rice, Philip Blair. "Edna Millay's Maturity," *Nation*, November 14, 1934.

Rosenfeld, Paul. "Under Angry Constellations," *Poetry*, October, 1939.

Schwartz, Delmore. "Poetry of Millay," *Nation*, December 18, 1943.

Sheehan, Vincent. *The Indigo Bunting*. New York: Harper & Bros., 1952.

Simonson, Lee. *Minor Prophecies*. New York: Harcourt, Brace and Co., 1927.

Van Doren, Carl. "Youth and Wings: Edna St. Vincent Millay," *Century*, June, 1923.

Wilson, Edmund. "Memoir; excerpt from *The Shores of Light*," *Nation*, April 19, 1952.

Yost, Karl. *A Bibliography of the Works of Edna St. Vincent Millay*. New York and London: Harper & Bros., 1937.

Index